D0030161

I WILL NEVER GIVE UP!

By Derek W. Clark

The true and inspiring story about a foster kid who found
the light at the end of the tunnel.

I WILL NEVER GIVE UP. COPYRIGHT © 2007 by Derek W. Clark. All rights reserved. This book may not reproduced, in whole or in part, in any form or by any means electronic or mechanical, include photocopying, recording, or by any information storage and retrieval system now known or hereafter invented, without written permission from the publisher.

Printed in the United States of America.

FIRST EDITION

I WILL NEVER GIVE UP
WRITTEN BY DEREK W.CLARK

WWW.IWILLNEVERGIVEUP.COM

CONTACT DEREK CLARK AT DEREK@IWILLNEVERGIVEUP.COM

Edited by Michael Laemmle
Email: mrlaemmle@gmail.com

Cover design by Adreana Shavers
WWW.BOLDGRAPHIXINC.COM

PUBLISHED BY NEVER LIMIT YOUR LIFE
OFFERING LIFE COACHING AND SEMINARS
To Book Life Coaching and Seminars call 1-800-980-0751

WWW.NEVERLIMITYOURLIFE.COM

ISBN 13: 978-0-615-17544-7

PREFACE

Dr. Ariane T. "Doc" Alexander
Military Psychologist
Foundation for Eternal Courage

As a military psychologist who specializes in PTSD and war trauma [both among active duty troops/veterans and civilian populations] my opening statement is that Derek's life, and self-actualized recovery, is a profile in eternal courage. Derek's early experiences suffered during his most formative years, from infant throughout childhood were equal in intensity to what a soldier goes through in a POW experience. My personal history includes being held hostage for ninety days by Islamist Extremist terrorists, suffering torture and daily threats of beheading, yet I can honestly say that my experience was *less* traumatic than what Derek went through in his early years—because I was an adult trained to handle the situation—and Derek was an infant/child—*with only a child's resources to handle a situation that was equal to a POW experience.*

As a psychologist, I feel I must speak out *against* the clinical diagnosis which was assigned to Derek Clark and offer testimony to put it into perspective.

As a psychologist I am in *complete agreement with Derek* that the use of labels on children, and subsequent pathologizing during diagnosis of children, can create a self-fulfilling prophecy and negative outcome. The criteria used to diagnosis children, does not allow for the 'courage factor' and what the human soul must do to survive an extreme experience—it, and the mental health community in general perpetually sees the glass as half empty rather than half full. For example, it has been well documented in neurological studies that psychosis can be transferred within environments and can be environmentally caused. Almost every human being, if placed in isolation for extended periods, will become psychotic. *Yet what is more traumatic than the emotional isolation of an abused foster child, who has no resources to fight back?*

It is important for all child abuse survivors to be told that testing is only as good as the diagnostic capability of the tester. Testing and subsequent diagnosis is an art form as well as a science. Most people daily graduate medical school and psychiatric school, *but it has been my experience only 10% can correctly diagnose*. To this psychologist, the majority of testers seem to be devoid of both compassion and common sense. Derek's clinical report states, "Before the testing even began, Derek told the Examiner that he had 'bionic powers and that he wanted to be on TV with the 'bionic man.' At times, Derek seemed unable to distinguish between reality and fantasy."—Good grief! All of us could imagine the excitement of an abused child, wanting to share the one thing that was giving him hope—his heroes—with someone he might have thought would listen, in speaking to someone he thought might be different than the abusers. Every child at that age, whether abused or not, has imagined he or she is a super hero.

And if for an abused child the fantasy becomes so real because of the longing to escape the reality—that is *not* pathology, *that is the human soul doing anything it can to survive.* Include in the mix the triple-headed serpent of child abuse, rejection and emotional isolation and frankly, even I as an adult would want to be Lara Croft, Tomb Raider. If I did *not* reach for a hero in the darkness and fantasize about being them, then I would be truly insane.

Fantasy is a child's way of coping, but fantasy is also a sign of high intelligence, *NOT* mental retardation. Fantasy is the child's way of keeping sanity during insane experiences or environments. And yet fantasy is a common factor in people who hold high levels of creative force—artists, writers, musicians, inventors, etc. Anyone who has ever enjoyed Derek's music would understand that in his category of music, he is a positive force and talent. I write this with tears in my eyes, I would have given anything to be his mother. To have the gifts Derek has, and to have gone through that early horrific beginning that he experienced, is a true atrocity.

As I write this, the stars are shining brightly against the Iraqi night. This evening I had read an excerpt of Derek's book to our platoon. During the reading it was so quiet out here in the remote desert area our FOB is located in, that we could literally hear the insects move about in the dark. Derek's words were so riveting that everyone seemed barely breathing, and time itself seemed to stop as I read Derek's words about his childhood. During the reading tears ran down my cheeks, and at one point I looked up and saw similar reactions in the rest of

the platoon. We all shed tears, but they were the good kind—
*the kind of tears that heal and are sent from God to let us
know He is hearing our prayers.* When I finished, the platoon
was silent for about five minutes, and they immediately
requested I reread the excerpt. Derek's words rang true for all
of them, for each of these young Marines had spent some or all
of their childhood in foster care, and had come from similar
situations of abuse, rejection and emotional isolation. Derek's
life is a profile in courage, and it touched every one of us to
the core.

I first heard of Derek when a friend gave me his CD titled
Good Night Soldier. As the Mother of four Marine sons who
were in harms way, and a Gold Star Parent whose oldest son
was KIA [Killed in Action], Derek's song, "Good Night
Soldier" became an anthem for me. Yet another track on this
CD titled "I Just Wanna Be A Kid" would make me weep,
because the poignancy of his voice during this song, and the
lyrics describing his tough childhood, touched a place within
me, so deep in my soul, it was like God touched me Himself.
I never knew my birth mother, and Derek's anguish was my
own. The power of music and the musician will always be the
universal language, and Derek possesses a super power in his
ability to touch the human soul through his music. Years later,
as I got to know Derek the person, and his reputation, and then
his history, I was extremely honored to write this preface to his
book.

When I read Derek's story, for me it was what I call a touchstone moment. To me touchstone moments are when

something inside a person, like the voice of a guardian angel, whispers *TAKE NOTE, THIS IS ONE OF THE MOST IMPORTANT MOMENTS ON EARTH, BECAUSE GOD IS PRESENT.* Touchstone moments to me are those moments that imprint at the deepest level on body, heart, mind, and soul. A person feels it in the visceral sense, the gut sense, that God is present. For anyone who has been a foster child, I know reading Derek's book will be a touchstone moment.

One of my very first touchstone moments was when I was six and saw the film *The Ten Commandments* with Charlton Heston. The entire film was riveting to me, even at six, but in two of the touchstone moments—scenes in the film where he saw the burning bush, and parted the red sea—it was as if time stopped, and I heard that angelic voice whisper... *TAKE NOTE, THIS IS ONE OF THE MOST IMPORTANT MOMENTS ON EARTH, BECAUSE GOD IS PRESENT.*

When I read Derek's book I hear that same angel, he again says, *TAKE NOTE, THIS IS ONE OF THE MOST IMPOR-TANT MOMENTS ON EARTH, BECAUSE GOD IS PRE-SENT. My heart, mind, soul and physical being can only say it is utterly important to the world that Derek write this book and share it with the world.*

To me, Derek's story is also about the human soul's ability to survive; his story is ultimately about courage.

To let the reader know how high up Derek is on my list of heroes, I will tell the following story....

The earliest intense experience of courage I can remember was when I was seven years old. My grandfather and I were in a village in Nigeria, where Grandfather, who worked for the World Health Order, had come to inoculate the children with vaccinations.

There were reports of a man-eating lion in the area, so everyone was on edge and we children were told to stay within the village. Like most kids, we did not listen, so I and my new-found African playmates ran off into the bush. A pack of hyena's were on the other side of the tall grass. An older boy had us gather rocks and all climb up in a tree where he taught us it was great sport to torment the pack with rock tosses. The pack went into a frenzy and it was bloody mayhem as they fought each other. We all felt bad at that point, knowing we did something bad hurting and agitating those animals. We were splattered with blood from the fight below, and then finally when the hyenas slunk off we ran back towards the village.

Smelling of blood we gave off a delicious scent to man-eating lions. NaTingGowah, was what the villagers called this particular man-eater lion. NaTingGowah smelled us and tracked us to the village. As we stood in the center of the village explaining ourselves, this man-eater ran in, scattering everyone in terror, and making the men run for their guns.

This lion squared off dead center with me. I looked into his eyes: golden, feral, possessing a soul deeper and more powerful than anything I would ever face later in life. A wildness, yet an intelligence, stared deeply into my eyes. I could smell the strong musk of the lion, and as he snuffed over me with his giant whiskers, the mist from his nostrils baptized me. He leaned back and roared, lashing his tail and tearing up chunks of the turf with taloned paws the size of dinner plates. His hot breath flowed over me like the fierce desert winds of Iraq. I was unable to move or to speak, but for some reason I was not afraid. I felt respect for the lion, but never fear. I heard St. Michael whisper in my ear, "Be not afraid, for the Lord is with thee." Perhaps it was my fearlessness that made NaTingGowah spare me. But I think it was God's presence and the presence of his holy angel.

NaTingGowah circled me three times, then lifted his left leg up and totally hosed me with his urine. That smell did not completely come off me for six months. Strangely, the lion then walked off. I went into shock for three days, in which I had many strange dreams. The medicine man of the village said I was singled out to be a warrior of the lion clan, that NaTingGowah had made me one of the 'lion people.'

They had a great initiation ceremony, and I at age seven was initiated into their lion clan.

And then when I got here to Iraq, Iraqi's began calling me Asad Baabill, which means Lion of Babylon, and to the local people this name is given to describe someone who is fearless in standing up to evil.

To me Derek Clark is the true Asad Baabill—his courage is equal to a Marine who must stand his ground to fight in a war zone, or a Marine who is taken hostage and must find a way to keep courage and survive. The "lion" Derek faced in writing about his intimate moments of his childhood are as real, and as terrorizing as the lion I faced as a child or the 'lion' I was forced to become to fight terrorism.

In my studies of PTSD and war trauma, the two states are identical in experience to survivors of child abuse and domestic violence. Yet to me, the experience of an abused child will always be the most severe of the two situations, because a child is fighting back with everything they have, without having been given the tools to fight in the first place.

Derek has a gift to reach out to other survivors of foster care, to heal them with his words and music, to be a force and a power for good in this world. The following story is an example of the healing force Derek gives to the world through his music.

I had the privilege to know one young Marine in Iraq that served under me, whose platoon name was Stryker, who had a similar horror-filled childhood to Derek's and, like Derek, grew up in foster care. Stryker was KIA 2007 in Iraq. When Stryker passed, he had put me down as his next of kin, and his journal passed to me. This is an entry he wrote regarding his experience of foster care and the effect of Derek's music on his soul:

"Damn Real, this probably was one of the best days of my life. War Dawg played this CD for me by a dude named Derek Clark, and the song was called *I Just Wanna Be A Kid*. Man, when I heard that song and listened to the words, I just totally felt like my soul was peeled back from my heart—

I just thought of every time I was abused as a child, and all the pain, feelings of lack of self-worth, and crushing sadness, isolation and depression—the ultimate hell of my childhood seemed to soar out of me with every note of that song. I just lost it. I cried like a baby but War Dawg was totally cool about it, and she and the Chaplain came over and talked to me. The whole time the song kept playing over and over in the background, because I had put it on repeat when I popped it into the CD player. I never told anyone nothing like what had happened to me as a kid, but Derek's song seemed to make it okay, and for the first time I was able to tell someone of the pain inside. Every time Derek's song spun around my head, it was like he was telling me, "It's okay man, let it out," and it was like another layer of pain was burnt off me.
For the first time in my life the pain had lifted, and it's because of that song. Then War Dawg told me that Derek had a childhood similar to mine, and I cried again. I hope some day I will get to meet Derek and tell him how great his music is and how it healed this one little boy hidden deep within a US Marine's body out here in the Iraqi sandbox."

Stryker, you are telling him now.

Derek I am so proud of you. So very proud. Congratulations on your outstanding book. On behalf of Stryker, from the US Marines, OOORAH, which is the highest compliment the Marines can offer.

SAEPIUS EXERTUS, SEMPER FIDELIS, FRATER INFINITAS... *[OFTEN TESTED, ALWAYS FAITHFUL, BROTHERS FOREVER].*

Dr. Ariane T. "Doc" Alexander

CONTENTS

WIFE'S ACKNOWLEDGEMENT

I will often jokingly say that Derek should come with a warning label on his forehead, stating "Beware! Has tendencies to cross the line!" What I lovingly mean is please don't be offended, he is really just expressing his thoughts. I know, what an anomaly! This really shouldn't be the case in our FREE society. We should be able to intelligently speak about all and any issues. We should not have to worry about being afraid of being labeled something terrible and offending someone.

In Derek's own style and honest words he has written about what bothers him most. He has personal experiences with being labeled and boxed in by what others think he should be and say. From the very beginning of his life he was labeled by his biological parents as no good and too much trouble. They thought they needed to physically beat that into him. They had no idea that he would choose to use those terrible experiences and make himself strong against any physical attacks. The "system" wanted to label him and box him in as a mentally handicapped child. They had no idea that Derek would choose to take the love and knowledge he received from his foster parents and make himself into an intelligent and lovable man.

There were many people in 1994 who thought when I married Derek—who had no job—that we might always struggle financially. But then again they had no idea that Derek would take on that fight and push himself to become a prominent and financially successful business owner and entrepreneur. It seems that Derek actually takes great pleasure in proving people wrong. He will not be stuck into the box of what others may think about him. He is a fighter and he works hard at whatever challenge comes his way.

Derek has also had some wonderful people who have helped him grow in his life, especially his loving foster parents. The unconditional love and support that was given to him has driven his desire to give back. He has this great desire to help others who may be lost or unappreciated. His song "Goodnight Soldier" partly came about because of the love he has for others and the families who have suffered such a great loss. It also came about because he wanted to do something for others and give in the only way he could—through music. I am in awe of how many people this song has comforted in their time of loss and distress. He has given so much through his music and now he wants to help others with his book. Through his difficult experiences and his fighting attitude I hope that others will become stronger and learn to never give up!!!

Derek is a loving and involved father to his three wonderful children, and I am thankful that I picked him out to be the father of our children. I am lucky to have such an incredible spouse to rely on and to comfort me with all of my needs. I love Derek and thank him for never giving up on us!

His loving wife,
Joy

MY DEDICATION

To my natural mother, thank you for giving me the precious gift of life and for giving me away so that I could have a better life. Although we don't talk, I want to let you know that it was a tough life for me. I was lonely and afraid. I felt like a lamb among wolves. I had to learn how to survive, and deal with what life handed me. It chokes me up thinking about it, but it keeps me real. I didn't always understand your reasons for doing what you did, but your true sacrifice has made me a passionate, empathetic, enduring, loving and determined man. I am a stronger man because of my suffering! I thank you for leaving me alone all those years so that I could find myself and grow without the mind-trip of holding onto the thought that you would come back for me. So many foster children get messed up because their Mom and Dad keep sticking their faces into the mix, giving the child false hopes that they are coming back for them—then never coming! Life becomes confusing and hopeless. I am truly thankful that you did not do that to me.

To my foster mother and foster father, I consider you my Mom and Dad. Thank you for your undying patience throughout the years. I thank you for leaving the TV off and for not having video games to play with (when all my friends had them), so that I could nurture my talents and abilities and turn into the hardworking and loving person you raised. Because of your discipline, laziness is not in my bones. I thank you for introducing me to animals, music, sports and Boy Scouts. Thanks for music camp too, and for cheering me on at those music competitions and sports events. I loved those command performances. We sure had some great times.

To my beautiful, angelic, and loving wife! You are amazing! Thanks for being my biggest cheerleader and for your incredible ability to be a great wife and an unbelievable mother. Your laughter and love inspires me. I love your gentleness, reassurance, your open mind, your unconditional love for me, and your acceptance of me as I am. I am so grateful that I met you and have been able to share my life with you.

To my beautiful children, Montgomery, Ozmond and Remington. I never thought children could bring so much joy and love into my life. The sight of your smiles makes the strongest man weak, as do the loving hugs and happy screams of "Daddy's home!" You are all amazing. You have brought me so many happy tears, so many smiles and bursts of laughter. You just make me melt. I never thought my love could be so strong. You are my blood and my heroes because you saved me from a poisonous past. I learn from you every day. You are the living proof that life makes me better as I go along.

To all the Foster Children and every child suffering in this world: TAKE A DEEP BREATH! This suffering is only one small part of your big, adventurous life. Don't let it consume your entire existence, and don't use it as an excuse for your downfalls. I know you may feel lost because nobody really wants to call you their own, but you have the power to take decisive actions and break the cycle of self-doubt. One day you will have the power to do right by creating a family of your own. That's what life is really about! You will make it if you surround yourself with good friends who make good choices and set good examples for you.

Your circumstances are not your fault. For many years I thought I was to blame for my parents giving me up. Later in life I realized it wasn't my fault. I WAS ONLY FIVE YEARS OLD! I was the kid and they were the adults. Don't let your emotions poison you. Don't be a nothing, be everything you want to be, and keep dreaming. Never let anybody tell you that you can't do something. Don't ever let anyone take your dreams away from you. Don't ever be a slave to drugs or alcohol; otherwise you are just another casualty. Use your experiences; they will make you mentally stronger than the average kid. Believe in yourself, bulletproof your soul.

At times loneliness is a virtue, it allows you to discover yourself. Don't ever, ever, hold back crying. It cleanses your soul. Don't forget to laugh. When I was going through rough times, the best medicine was laughter. I've always liked being the clown.

Don't hate, that is the real poison. Learn to forgive. Secretly, I nurtured a lot of poisonous feelings throughout my life. These intense feelings were the fire that drove my desire to prove to the world that I wasn't "a nobody." I think sometimes I tortured my own soul and liked it. If there is one thing I have learned, it is this: If I Can Fly, You Can Fly. Let your spirit fly so that you may one day help another person! Never Give Up!!!

Under 1 year old

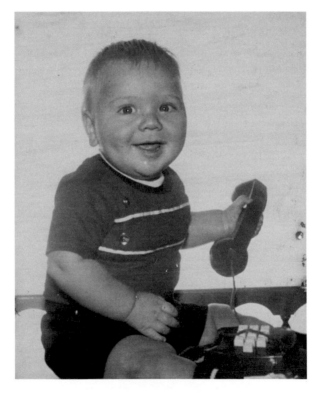

1 year old

1 year old

2 years old

2 years old

4 years old

4 years old

6 years old

6 years old

MY SAD EARLY LIFE WAS BUT A STEPPING STONE TO A HAPPY AND FULFILLING LIFE

This is the true story of my life. A life in which abuse, loneliness, and dark nights of despair rattled the very bones of my body, drained the tears of my spirit, shattered my mind into a million fragments, and left me for awhile plodding through life as an empty shell, a lost and helpless soul. I have breathed the air of the unloved, and suffered deep psychological and spiritual wounds due to abandonment at an early age by my mother and father. I have blamed myself for a past over which I had no control. My trust in people was displaced with hostility and anger. And yet, *my spirit would not be broken.* I have fought for survival in the name of love, powered by a dogged will whose voice never stopped telling me to NEVER GIVE UP!

I was a five year-old kid, and already a survivor of appalling events. I have never known my father. My mother, having given up on me, placed me in the County Social Services Foster Care System. She was desperate to be rid of me. The saddest, most inexplicable part of this was that she kept my younger brother and older sister. I was devastated knowing I had been deleted from my family. I was now motherless and fatherless. I loved my mother, brother and sister, but my love for them wasn't enough for her to keep me in the family.

She claimed she could not control me, and that I was a "devil," but I now know she was the one out of control. I was the child and she was the adult. I am not to blame for the predicament I found myself in. That is life; it is unfair.

There are millions of kids who have been given up on, and I hold their parents completely responsible. The ignoble actions of parents will always be remembered by their children. I know, because that five year-old foster child still lives within me, constantly striving to be empowered, to make his insecurities my own. But I refuse to be a victim; I am a conqueror. I am stronger than my unworthy parents!

There is no question; the mental and physical struggles of my life have proved very difficult to overcome. They say the first five years of a child's life are the most critical to his or her development, and that children soak up everything they experience like a sponge. I agree. I have seen my own three children sponge both my strengths and weaknesses. Kids watch their parents, and mimic what they observe. The influence of my first five years contributed to many destructive behaviors throughout my life. I often wished I had been given away at birth, so that I wouldn't have had to endure the memories and nightmares which have haunted me these many years.

There is always a lesson to be learned from adversity. I have learned many such lessons the hard way, but have found there is a light at the end of the tunnel. The light that leads us out of the darkness is the positive energy that comes to surround those who continually search for what life has to offer.

The answer is always within. By harnessing this positive energy you can accomplish anything. Nothing has ever held me back from "going for it." I have not let anyone or anything stop me from making my dreams a reality. I keep on keeping on. I am an unstoppable force. I am headstrong and know exactly what I want. I have always trusted my intuition.

My search for life's meaning eventually brought me through a baptism by fire, which cleansed my soul. I am like the mystical "Phoenix" that has risen from its own ashes, a resurrected soul, a lost boy who evolved into a man. In life's journey, I was meant to shine.

It is this journey in which fractured souls are made whole again. It is this journey in which wounds are healed and pain is finally replaced with love and peace.

This is a bitter-sweet story filled with real blood, real tears, unthinkable pain, turmoil, hope, love, success; and finally, significance. This is the true story of a fearless boy who fought for his life and won.

This book is for anyone who is suffering emotionally, mentally, and physically in their life. I am not a doctor, nor do I hold a degree in psychology. I can't claim to have graduated from a prestigious university with a 4.0 G.P.A. I am not here to "fix" you or put your life together in the way I see fit, I am here to help you first identify, and then to *modify* your thought processes. Unhappy thoughts lead to unhappy actions, with the end result being an unhappy life. We all want a happy life and peaceful state of mind. I believe that what you think you are or can be, you have the power to be. The challenge is to become the person you want to be.

My credentials are relevant, credible and simple. They are "real life" disasters and triumphant experiences. I am in touch with my inner self and thought that now, having overcome, I would take the opportunity to share my experiences; those experiences which I have survived, and how I have thrived in spite of them. We are all imperfect and sometimes choose to unwisely focus on our suffering. We become attached to our pain, making it a part of who we are. But there comes a time when we can no longer relinquish our minds and bodies to the victim mentality. We must become mind-conquerors.

A person doesn't need a college degree to deeply touch another's soul. We are all human and feel emotions, whether it is fear, love, happiness, anger or sadness. People can make an impact on others in dramatic, life-changing ways, both negative or positive.

Your life has meaning! You are significant! You are who you want to be! Believe that! There is a real price to pay for a true smile, the kind that will shine forth from within you, but it's a price worth paying!

YOUR LIFE IS THE ATTITUDE
FOUND IN YOUR HEART!

Take a moment to answer the following questions. Consider what they might reveal about your life.

Have you felt rejected?
Do you feel like you are not worth loving?
Is it hard for you to love? To trust?
Does someone's love, or lack thereof, determine your self-worth?
Do you blame yourself for the bad things which have happened in your life?
Do you sabotage yourself?
Are you plagued with doubts?
Have you felt alone?
Do you believe that God does not know you or love you?
Do you lack faith?
Ever considered suicide?
Do you allow yourself to be victimized?
Allow your past to control who you are today?
Does fear keep you from taking actions that would place you closer to where you want to be in life?
Are you fearful of making new friends?
Do you thrive on negativity?
Have you lost a loved one and wondered how you could go on?

Are you an orphan? Or a foster child?
Do you have an out-of-control child?
Were you adopted?
Are you a foster mother or foster father?
Has your mother ever given you away?
Did your father walk away when you were born, never to come back?
Do you feel others have labeled you?
Are you living up to the label?
Did you grow up with a stepmother, stepfather, and stepfamily?
Have you experienced child abuse?
Do you have a learning disability?
Do you feel lost and without purpose?
Have you been given up on?
Have you been close to giving up?
Have you given up?
Have you let depression take control of your life?
Have you cried hysterically on the bathroom floor?
Have you let anger fill your heart?
Have you suffered panic-attacks so severe that if you didn't consciously force yourself to breathe, you thought you'd die?
Does anxiety keep you from being the best you can be?
Have you given up on making your dreams realities?

FREE YOURSELF FROM THE MINDSET WHICH HAS BOXED YOU IN! THERE IS NO BOX! LIFE IS LIMITLESS!

It is my hope that this book will inspire you to take control of your thoughts and enjoy a fulfilling life, no matter how difficult your situation is. You will learn how I succeeded with a "realistic" positive attitude, and how you can survive ups and downs by not succumbing to the mental trap of negativity. You will find that simply forcing yourself to be positive is not enough. It can send a person into a fluctuating "positive/negative" or "happy/sad" state of mind. I call it the Paddle-Ball Effect. You're up one day and down the next. The harder you try to create a false, deceptively positive attitude, the further down the mind's negative tendencies will bring you. This unhealthy cycle of emotional ups and downs can become a difficult habit to break.

This mindset actually serves to make a person sadder in the long run, because they come to feel as if they're incapable of letting genuinely positive energy flow through and from themselves. More often than not, the individual finally gives up, allowing their weaknesses to take control of them. We see something similar occur with the Yo-Yo dieting routine.

You have the strength to make it through the ups and down of your life without going to these emotional extremes. Having a balanced life is an attainable goal, and has always been a goal of mine. This book has a purpose, which is to help people overcome their limiting and negative thoughts. It will demonstrate how procrastination steals your time. It will inspire the courage take action. You will learn the four letter word you can say over and over again for inner strength. It will show you how I used the POWER of taking ACTION in my life, and how you can take action in yours. It will show you how a mind-conqueror survives and thrives from the battle within. It will encourage you to improve your business and personal life through clear and lucid thinking. It will help you develop trust in yourself and give you the confidence needed to overcome.

We have all been engaged in a war with ourselves at one time or another. Now is the time for rethinking our strategies and winning the war once and for all. You must grow beyond your limiting thoughts, and have the courage and conviction to tell yourself "I WILL NEVER GIVE UP!"

"Living in the past is kind of like living in a coffin...it's totally constraining, and ends up being a lid on your growth..." -- Doug Firebaugh

I

Someone aware of possessing a personal individuality

(Merriam- Webster Dictionary)

WILL

Determination, Insistence, Persistence
The Power Of Control Over One's Actions Or Emotions
(Merriam-Webster Dictionary)

NEVER

Not Ever-Not Under Any Condition
(Merriam-Webster Dictionary)

GIVE

To Put Into The Possession Of Another For His Or Her Use
(Merriam-Webster Dictionary)

UP!

In Or Into A Higher Position Or Level,
Into A State Of Greater Intensity Or Excitement

(Merriam-Webster Dictionary)

Why I Wrote This Book

The message of this book is for everyone, though the book itself is intended for readers aged fourteen and up. I desired it be written in a style simple enough that people of almost any age could read it and relate to the story, in the hope that they be inspired to evaluate and, if need be, change their life, no matter how daunting their circumstances. Our choices determine our outcomes. If one makes good choices, one will never give up, and choosing to never give up is the first and most important choice one makes. The world will often impose its own idea of who you are and who you can be, but don't succumb to those judgments. You are who you decide you will be. You have the power, don't relinquish it. Strength comes from taking action. Adversity makes the strong stronger and the weak weaker.

I consider my actions and thoughts to be those typical of a strong person, but I wasn't always strong. A difficult early life made me the man I am today. This book will take you on a journey through my life. It is a collection of thoughts, case histories, poems, journal entries, lessons I have learned as a father, and song lyrics, many written in my darkest and loneliest hours. These are my reactions to the struggles life has thrown at me.

I won't lie and tell you I was the happiest kid. I struggled mentally and physically. There were traumatic experiences throughout my youth and I had to learn to live with them. I was given up by my own Mom at an early age, yet inexplicably she kept my brother and sister. I was so scared and alone, and these feelings persisted on through my teenage years.

This negative energy wasn't channeled into depression and melancholy. I wasn't a depressed kid who was weak and picked on. I actually went the opposite way, and was filled with aggression and anger.

The fact is, I was a very angry kid with problems trusting, loving, and accepting others. These difficulties are described in the journal entries which I made throughout the first twenty years of my life. Deep down I believe I was a happy kid, whose anger and mistrust arose from the miserable life experiences which I had to endure at such a young age.

A fire raged within me. I could no longer trust adults and constantly defied authority, always eager to challenge the wisdom of my elders. I was not fearful, I was fearless, albeit not always in a healthy way. Some deep mistrustful instinct was triggered inside me, and knowing I could no longer trust adults, I felt I had to survive on my own and could only trust myself. While other kids were happy with their families, I was with foster families who often provided me little more than a bed to sleep on and food to eat. I knew these families weren't my real one, and the parents weren't my real Mom and Dad. Nor did I ever really know how long I might be at a particular foster home. This uncertainty kept me constantly on edge.

I was hurt deeply when my mother abandoned me to the foster care system. If I couldn't trust my own mother, how could I trust anyone else? It brings tears to my eyes even now as I write this book, remembering the child I was, unable to trust another living person. I was a five year-old kid who was about to learn the art of mental survival on his own.

It is my hope that through this book, I will both bring healing to myself and inspire others to find the strength within, the power necessary to thrive, to keep despair and loneliness at bay, and not allow these destructive habits of mind to take you down a road of perpetual self-torture. It is unfortunate, but it seems we humans like to torture ourselves by blaming our-selves for the circumstances of our life, and those aspects of it that seem beyond our control. But life is out of control. The only thing we can control is our attitude. That is it! Life is what happens when you're making other plans, but we own our thoughts and control our outlook on life.

It is we who are capable of not letting it bite us or get the best of us. The strength and will to survive each day comes from within, and we can approach life with an attitude of gratitude.

It is a choice to be strong. It's that simple. We choose to stop the self-torture, and it is ourselves who free us from our mental prisons. We often keep ourselves from doing great things and put up imaginary walls to block us in. But we can just walk out the imaginary door. There is always a door for walking in, just as there is always an exit door for walking out. The mind always seeks an exit strategy. But you have to find it where it is hidden amongst all the mental clutter. Don't ever tell yourself there is no way out of your present situation. Remember, you are in control. Your thoughts are under your control. And when you take control of your thoughts, you can build the life you've always wanted.

It is my deepest hope that this book will inspire you to Never Give Up! Never succumb to the negative thoughts which may be weighing down your life. Thoughts are very heavy and can give you a false outlook on life. The "victim mentality" is one of the worst things that can enter a person's mind. It will change you mentally, physically, spiritually, and financially. Not only that, but you could very well pass this destructive mindset on to your children, just like any disease. The sins of the father are visited on the son.

By setting the good example of personal strength, by having control of your attitude and thoughts, you and your family will benefit. Do not come down with the "poor-me syndrome." Everyone has the fire and desire within to succeed in every aspect of their life. Cultivate your strength by believing in the power of Determination, Perseverance and Endurance.

IT IS NOT MY FAULT!

I have had a very eventful life filled with sadness, madness and joy. I can smile now, but try telling the five year-old kid inside of me to smile. It's still hard for me to smile while revisiting my younger years. It's as if my life were caught up in a tornado, all of my thoughts going in circles and being tossed around in every direction. The physical, mental, and emotional pain was all very real. Even if this little kid stands cold-faced and fearless in front of me now, it wasn't always that way.

I do not seek to paint my mother as a bad or evil person. I know now that she did what she had to do to survive. I may not be happy about it because as a little kid I paid the price for her choices, whether good or bad. But I have to say I am happy with who I am today, and this in part allows me to forgive her.

I was born in the year 1970. I almost wasn't born though. My mother was married and had a daughter, my older sister, before she was divorced. She met my biological father and became pregnant with me. He was not happy that she was pregnant. She was a hardworking waitress trying to support her daughter and soon-to-be-born son. When she was seven months pregnant, my father came in to the diner where she worked and

19

took her to the kitchen, where he beat her up, kicking her in the stomach several times in an attempt to kill her unborn baby (me). He was yelling about not wanting the baby. He was enraged that she planned to keep it. After that moment she feared for both her life and mine, and decided to hide from him.

I was born a healthy ten pound baby. I was just a big, pudgy infant. According to my mother I was born with a strong will, which became stronger as I grew into a toddler. It seems my willfulness was too much for her to handle, especially in light of the various insecurities in both her life and personality. Out of concern for my safety, she decided not to give me my father's last name for fear that he might one day find and kill me. She also decided to move from the town in which she was then living. But soon after I was born, my father did find us at her house, and threatened to kill me. She blocked his way to protect me, and he hit and kicked her. He then smashed the top off a beer bottle and held the sharp edge to my mother's throat. He said he would kill both of us.

I asked my Mom what attracted her to this monster, and she said that he was charming, tall, and very good-looking. He was much older than her, loved music, and was a sergeant in the United States Army. He had served in World War II. She later heard from his parents that his sanity was affected after his tank was hit by artillery. He barely survived the explosion. He lived but those who knew him later said his mind sometimes didn't work right, and he often became very violent. There is some speculation that the war left him shell-shocked, or with Post Traumatic Stress Disorder.

I realize that my mother did the best she possibly could, even though there were many mishaps. I know she was under a tremendous amount of stress having three children from three different fathers. The financial burden left her wondering how she was going to pay for these kids. It must have been over-whelming. Sometimes people just want security and I believe this is what my mother finally found with my stepfather. Even though I loathed him as the primary reason for her getting rid of me, he did provide her and her newborn with a certain amount of stability.

I am not here to blame my mother, or to make her feel guilty for her "sins." We are all sinners. I no longer judge her or hold her accountable for the hell I went through. It is hard to for-give and move forward with one's life. But I have always moved forward, and that is why I am where I am in life. I am not, nor have I ever been, a drug addict, alcoholic, or convict. I could have taken the easy way out and played the victim, but I guarantee I would not be where I am today if I had taken that path.

I have done great things with my life, but I have always been troubled by questions that I needed to ask my mother. Why did you give me up and keep my brother and sister? Why did you hurt me? Why did you not come back for me? Why didn't you stay in touch with me more throughout my life? Where is my real father? Who is he? In the end, it was my county case files that finally provided the answers to these questions.

Looking back, the questions weren't really as important as I thought they were. I made it through life without knowing the answers, and I turned out remarkably well compared to others in similar situations. But I dwelt on these questions for years because I felt the need to be validated, when in reality the only person that needed to validate me was me.

THE GOODBYE

Here I was, a child desperate for love and affection, a scared little boy who was getting ready for what would be the longest ride of his life. I can't say I remember the drive to the orphanage, or the place where kids were stored, but I do remember not bringing along any toys. I remember the sun being out and the sky being blue. The day was pleasant, warm, and peaceful, in stark contrast to the foreboding anxieties that were raging inside me. I didn't know where I was being taken, only that this day would likely be the darkest of my life. The "longest ride" eventually ended at a place I considered an orphanage. It was a big building with lots of space and rooms. I figured it was an orphanage because all I saw were homeless and unloved kids. Kids who were no longer wanted by their Moms and Dads. I could see the sadness and fear in their eyes, and imagined that same fear must be showing in mine. We were now disposable, kids who could be thrown away or tossed overboard, never to be loved or comforted by our parents again.

Seriously, who would have cared if we were drowned or burned to death? At this point, it was already like we were being buried alive. We were being killed, suffocated, by lack of love. We were now the county's worry, pain and nightmare. My parents had given up! They were weak, and now I had to somehow become strong and survive. I felt deep misgivings and anxiety, the memories were killing me. I kept thinking, 'Where is my big sister?' I thought that surely she would come and rescue me because she loved me. I expected her to show up at any minute. But nobody came! Here I was, a helpless little five year-old boy, and my heart no longer beat for anybody but myself. Hope was lost for me at that point.

I don't even remember seeing my mother's eyes, or her giving me one final hug, or her even saying something as simple as "I love you Derek," or, "I will be back for you son." How could she not even give me a goodbye hug? She was the one who had placed both herself and me in this position.
I was the son, paying the price for all of her bad choices. She could have at least said, "Well, take care Derek, I love you." Or how about just a few basic words of tenderness and encouragement? "You will make it through this Derek." Even something negative, critical, or hurtful would have been better than nothing: "I blame you for all of this," or "Derek, you are the devil," or "Derek, I hate you for what you have become," or "Derek, you forced me to do this, I blame you!" But NO, nothing was said, and the indifferent silence was more painful than any words could have been, no matter how angry or loveless.

I guess it wasn't like she was wishing me well as I went off to college. I'm sure she quickly got rid of me in order to avoid the emotional impact of her actions, of seeing herself throwing away her own blood, her selfish desire to choose her husband over me, her son. But as her blood son, I probably reminded her of past mistakes, of the regretful choice she made to start a romantic relationship with my biological father. I have no doubt my stepfather comforted her, and told her she was making the right choice in giving her son away. Even as a little boy, I was certain he had been the one pushing to give me away. He was a piece of crap! No doubt he still is today. He broke up our family. I hoped that every day after he gave up me he lived a life of hell, and that when he died, hell would take him back. My Mom used to call me the devil, but as far as I could see, she'd married the devil. She got it all mixed up. Mother, you married the devil.

After she dropped me off, my little life as a boy who nobody could or would love began. At this time, I wasn't even able to love this little boy. Plagued with insecurities and doubts about my self-worth, I was now going to have to make a home here in hell. I was left alone with all the bigger boys, who just stared at me like wolves salivating at their thoughts of feasting on a weak, vulnerable little lamb. I was the proverbial sheep being lead to the slaughter.

I was very alert and very scared. Very, very, very scared! A woman took me into another room and showed me around. It technically wasn't an orphanage, but there was very little difference between an orphanage and whatever this place was. Besides, what difference did it make? It was an imposing, overwhelming, cold, impersonal and institutional building. There was no love here. This was a place of pain and ghosts. We were throwaways or misfits. Possibly we were angels who nobody recognized as such, but that could hardly have occurred to us at the time. This was to be my new home while a new family was being prepared for me. I didn't know who or what kind of people might invite me to share in their life. Or for that matter, if anybody would want me at all.

I remember thinking that my Mom would of course be coming back for me. I could care less about my stepfather, but I trusted that my mother's love would override whatever other concerns she had. I felt a deep hatred for my stepfather. He had taken my Mom away from me. If she didn't come back, I placed the blame squarely on his shoulders. I cried from loneliness and fear.

The older boys were antagonizing and threatening me, trying to push my limits. I got angry and taunted them back, so one of the boys pulled out a toothbrush with the end sharpened for use as a weapon. I ran for my life. I thought I was going to die. I knew what death was even at a young age. According to the county reports I had a kind of morbid fascination with death. Later that night, when it got dark, I grew even more frightened. It became obvious that if my mother was going to come back for me, it wouldn't be any time soon.

We slept in what appeared to me like a giant classroom with a bunch of beds placed in it. It was some kind of enormous warehouse for storing kids. I remember hearing lots of crying in the middle of the night, puncturing through the silence. Other kids were missing their Moms and Dads, brother and sisters. Where were mine? I wondered why my brother and sister got to stay with our mother and I was stuck here in this sad, terrible place. Why was I rejected and deleted from the family? Was I special somehow, or was I just a piece of garbage? Why couldn't I just be a normal kid like others? A kid who had a family? Why didn't anyone love me? Why couldn't I just be a kid?

MY LIFE AS A 5 YEAR-OLD, THROUGH THE EYES OF AN ADULT

When I was five years-old it was a crazy time for me. I figure instead of trying to recall everything and explain my behavior in my own words, I prefer to let the adults in my life paint the picture of what was going on. This is just one of the reports which labeled and diagnosed me. Additional reports are in the appendix at the back of the book. They are the reports which decided my fate, but my fate was destined to be different than what their diagnoses implied. This information is very revealing about my childhood. It should be understood that I was a product of my environment. All I wanted was to be a kid and be with my family. All of a sudden I was getting diagnosed and mentally picked apart like some lab monkey or diseased mouse. I felt like a medical experiment. When you read these, you will see that I was just a little boy who was very conscious of what was going on. After I first read these reports, I was very sorry for that little boy who they were diagnosing, trying to get inside his head. It took a couple of days for me to get over the sadness I felt for him. I could not believe this little boy was me. I have three little children of my own, and can't imagine having people pick them apart in order to ascertain where they should be placed in the world, all according to impersonal professional standards.

For those who have a child, try visualizing him or her at five years old in a similar situation. A situation, in which he or she feels completely alone, unsafe, unprotected, and Mommy or Daddy are not there to comfort. I remember some of these evaluations and how I behaved.

I am a fighter by nature and early on showed signs of stubbornness in doing what I wanted and refusing to acknowledge another's opinion of me. This tendency has carried on throughout my life. I do everything "Derek's way." I felt like the world was against me and that nobody liked me. I felt like I was totally backed into a corner, and the only way for me to let others know I was a real kid was to come out swinging.

Derek's Way may not always be the quickest or best way, but it's an eventful and adventurous way, and it has gotten me to the point in life where I am now. I love the place where the road of life has finally brought me. What a great destination. I believe my past was instrumental in bringing me to this moment, where I enjoy who I am and live a life full of enthusiasm. What you are about to read is the real deal.

REPORT FOR THE COUNTY JUVENILE COURT
July 8, 1976

The mother describes Derek's father as an ex-convict and an alcoholic, with severe emotional problems. The mother lost contact with Derek's father soon after the child's birth, but believes he returned to prison shortly thereafter for involvement in several armed robberies.

PSYCHOLOGICAL INFORMATION:

A verbal report from the doctor states that while the boy is not overtly psychotic, there is indication of this potential. The child laughs inappropriately and shows great anxiety. He is very suspicious of people and holds back as if fearful of making a mistake. Derek reminds his mother of his father and this causes her to reject Derek in many ways. He needs further testing to more accurately determine his I.Q. **He does not recognize such words as "dog, boy, cat."**

PARENTS STATEMENT:

After being advised of their rights, Derek's mother and stepfather stated that the minor has experienced emotional problems since the age of eighteen months. They stated that during the past year the minor's behavior has grown virtually unmanageable at times. They stated that he was unable to finish his kindergarten year in school because of problems he experienced with the other children and the disruptive behavior he demonstrated.

The parents state that the boy is hyperactive and that when he becomes involved in an activity which might endanger him or others around him, he will not respond to reasonable directions to stop this negative type of behavior. The parents further state that the minor must be physically restrained, and that he frequently flies into rages and is completely unmanageable.

On more than one occasion in the past year, the minor has been observed to pound his head on the floor. The parents further state that they cannot tolerate this behavior and the mother is fearful of hitting the child and injuring him. The stepfather states that the minor will not respond to his directions nor will the minor respond to the directions of the older sibling in the home. The parents believe that the minor must be supervised closely at all times and they are not capable of this level of supervision. At the present time, the parents have indicated that they are "unwilling" to participate in a program of counseling because they do not believe counseling will help solve the minor's behavior problem. The parent's were referred to this agency by the Psychiatric Emergency Unit.

PLACEMENT PLANS:

Emergency Foster Home Mother states that Derek is more physically aggressive than other children. She states that Derek is affectionate. Derek first went to the Emergency Foster Home on June 18th, 1976 and has remained there except for an eight day period when he returned to his parent's care. A sense of affection has developed between Derek and his Foster Parents.

FATHER:

Derek's father's whereabouts are unknown. He has not seen Derek since Derek was nine months old. **The last information the mother had on the father was that he was in an institution for the criminally insane.**

MOTHER AND STEPFATHER:

Mother and stepfather continue to have problems that make it difficult for them to deal with Derek. Mother does not show an ability to deal with or help resolve Derek's problems. Stepfather has mainly felt that the problems mainly experienced were Derek's and not his. He was not willing to participate in therapy. In considering whether or not Derek should return home, his decision was based on whether Derek has changed.

Since the jurisdictional court hearing, the mother and stepfather were originally planning on Derek's returning home after the school year. They saw out of home placement as a temporary plan to give Derek time to change his unmanageable behavior, and to give them time to consider how they might better deal with Derek. However in March, 1977 they decided they were unable to consider Derek's return. They felt, based on Derek's behavior during their visits, that he had not changed and they were unable to cope with his behavior. The parents appear to have very little willingness to use any counseling resources. They also declined the suggestion of parenting classes.

As an alternative to family restoration, they requested Derek be referred for adoption. However, the adoptions department was unable to accept this referral based on the severity of Derek's emotional problems. Guardianship was suggested as an alternative plan and the parents were in agreement. Following their decision, they have chosen not to visit Derek.

Derek:

Derek is described as a child with emotional problems. Neurological, psychological and learning disability evaluations were done on Derek. **Neurological tests indicate he is functioning on a normal 2 to 4 year old level, they indicate "mild retardation".** The psychological examination done for the Learning Disability Evaluation diagnose Derek as having Aretic Psychosis. It appears many of these problems are associated with his family. Both foster homes have reported problems with Derek's encopretic and eneuretic behavior, but this behavior is noticed only occasionally when Derek is under stress. The current foster family reports that Derek's behavior was the most difficult to deal with during the time the parents were visiting.

34

Derek seems to accept not returning to his mother's home and remaining with the foster family. He does ask about his mother and asks for visits with her but has not asked about returning home.

PLACEMENT REVIEW:

Special placement problems are hyperactive, emotionally disturbed youngster. **Neurological tests indicate "mild retardation".** Derek is having difficulty adjusting to school. Although he has adjusted well to this emergency foster home, the foster mother reports he gets upset by the other foster children leaving.

WORDS THAT KILL THE SPIRIT

As you can see from the reports, a lot of effort was put into describing my personality and mental capacity. One of the most disturbing words the doctor used was "retarded." I believe that this word, along with loser, stupid, and dumb, are some of the most damaging words in the English language. These words are extremely harmful to kids. What we think we can become, we usually can become. I believe labeling a child can become a self fulfilling prophecy. If a child is constantly getting cut down and labeled, I believe he will lose the will to try and become something better than expected. Yes, I had slowness in development and yes, I had a lot of emotional problems. But if everyone hastily slaps a label on a child, he or she will eventually live up to that characterization. How can somebody grow if it's already assumed their growth is stunted? This applies not only to children of all ages, but adults as well. We all need positive reinforcement. Don't let anyone's thoughts identify us and tell us what our limits are. Don't let anyone design you and fill your head with doubt, you stand up proud and determined to become the architect of your mind and soul. You are the master of your own mind.

These hurtful words do not uplift children. They are meant to demoralize them and make them feel like lesser beings. Even when kids joke about being a "retard" or say "I am dumb," or,

"You are stupid," it gradually instills that negativity in their minds. The result is that oftentimes kids will grow to fit that label. Their mental hard drive is being programmed, and these labels and words may never be erased. If you assimilate these limiting, destructive words, you may start believing what they imply.

And if everyone else believes in their accuracy, it can lead to various forms of self-destruction. You can see it in kids suffering from low self-esteem and lack of confidence. They just might be living up to a label somebody else has applied to them. What labels have you allowed to characterize yourself or your children? This labeling could have damaging effects throughout their life.

If I had known how I was labeled as a child, I know I would have turned out very differently, and would possibly be in prison or even dead. Don't let anyone use a label to turn you into something you are not.

I dislike the word "retarded." I believe mentally-challenged children are angels sent from Heaven to teach us the virtues of love, appreciation, sacrifice and selflessness. I have more respect for mentally-challenged people who overcome great obstacles than "normal, high-achieving" individuals. These special, mentally-challenged individuals are a gift. They are great teachers. We can all learn from them. Anyone with a disability is here to enrich our lives. Respect them, watch and listen to them. Even though some are unable to speak, we can still learn a lot from their silence. We are all connected as human beings.

If your soul is open, it will allow you to see the little miracles working throughout our daily lives in mysterious ways.

A NEW FOSTER HOME ON A FARM

Here is a paper I found in my journal from my teenage years as a foster kid. I wrote about my experience living on a farm with lots of animals. I love animals and the spirit of healing they bring to us. Animals are so in tune to the human spirit. As a foster child, they helped me learn how to love again when I felt no one loved me. Horses are an amazing animal with feelings that can sense our sadness. As animals, they have special unique abilities to teach by example, how to love unconditionally, and heal the spirit of a wounded child.

"As I lay in my hammock swinging in a grove of eucalyptus trees, the clean, fresh, sinus-cleaning scent sifts through my nose and I am able to reminisce about some of my greatest memories. They are still so vivid, and will be forever. Who can ever forget the combined smell of corn husks, pine and eucalyptus trees, beautiful flowers and roses touched off with the sounds and odors of our farm animals? The smell of horse and goat manure used as fertilizer for the plants is drowned out by the sweet aroma of the beautiful flowers and the roses which attract honeybees. On the other hand, the manure attracts the flies. What a small price to pay for the setting of beautiful memories!

"I remember the early mornings. I would have to wake up and go into the horse pasture and help my dad shovel horse manure into the pickup truck. That was easy compared to going into the goat pen and carrying out loaded buckets and garbage cans full of goat manure. The main problem was that the pen was not a flat piece of land, it was at a tilt. So it was a little harder to carry the buckets out. Sometimes my parents would pay me twenty-five cents for each bucket I filled. Getting paid was nice, but I also enjoyed the fruits of my labor when eating fresh apples, zucchini, corn, string beans, cantaloupes, squash, broccoli and tomatoes.

"There's nothing like biting into a fresh cob of corn and having the kernels pop as you chomp down. Then there were the good old family picnics where we would all saddle up our horses and ride to Garin Ranch and partake of hamburgers, hotdogs, Jell-O, and cookies.

"My foster Mom would usually drive the car to the park and meet us there in order to have the hamburgers ready when we rode in starving for food. The ride was about two hours and the horses were grateful for the break as we ate.
At home I was responsible for breaking in (training) one of our ponies. His name was Bootie, an American white pony, very large and ready to take anybody for the wild ride of their life.

"I calmed him down after getting bucked off several times. It takes a lot of courage for a young boy to get back on a pony after being bucked off. Now he is a fast, smooth and well-disciplined ride.

"In the early morning I would get up and milk the goats. We had five that were milking and they would give about two-and-a-half gallons total. After milking, I would come into the house and filter the milk, put the date on the bottle and refrigerate it. Any effort was worth some fresh goat milk. I loved having a fresh glass of goat milk with chocolate chip cookies.

" I come from a foster family of seven kids and sometimes there would be a few extra foster children. I think my mother and father's door is always open for a lost kid who needs good, loving parents. The atmosphere when I walk into my house is cheerful, with the helping hand of Mom and Dad.

"Materially, the furniture is beat down, the carpet has been trod on over a million and a half times. The kitchen table is large enough for an army. There are toys lying around for people to walk on and break. It is not as clean as other people's houses, but what can you expect when you come from a large family who rides horseback, takes care of farm animals, plays in acres of dirt, goes dirt-bike riding, builds massive forts, climbs trees, and takes apart greasy motor parts. After all this we come into the house and sit down. One just can't have classy, expensive stuff when they live like that.

"I wouldn't give up this place for anything, because we as a family have made this house our home, full of love and closeness. Special family ties have been made that will never be broken. There are too many memories to recall on paper, but I can say one thing: a home like this makes the grouchiest people smile because it's a true fairy-land."

AN ANGRY KID

Here is a journal entry from a talk I gave in church when I was twelve years old.

"I have a goal. I am working on becoming more like Jesus. One of my problems is losing my temper. When a person gets mad and loses control of himself, bad things often happen.

"Lots of times we have to decide if we are going to let people or things make us lose control of ourselves. We do have the power to decide whether we will let ourselves become angry or not.

"When we get mad at our brother or sister, we act differently than when we get mad at our parents or teachers. You don't hit your teachers or parents, but brothers and sisters are often fair game.

"When I was about eight years old, I started getting warts on my hands. Now these weren't little warts. They were big warts. They just got bigger and bigger. It was crazy and embarrassing. I hated them. Kids at school used to make me mad when they would call me "Wartman". They would see me coming and say "Oh here comes the Wartman". I couldn't help it. I went to the doctor and every time they burned one off, a bigger one took its place. At one time, I had over 100 of the ugly things. I used to get mad and lose my temper and do terrible things and end up getting a detention. I would have to stay after school and that made me madder.

"Several years ago, I got mad at my older brother Colin when he was wrestling with me. He hurt me so I took revenge and punched a hole in his fish tank and cut my arm very badly. It was a bloody mess. I had cut a blood artery. Blood was spurting out like crazy. It was like a geyser. It was a mess for a long time and meant that I couldn't do a lot of fun things that summer.

"Then last year I got into a fight with a kid at school. He kept bugging me and bugging me until I got so mad that I broke a school window. I had to pay for it and it wasn't cheap.

"I was a little lucky because the Principal Mr. Cox let me work it off by helping the janitor clean up the school. I hate to clean toilets.

"I know God loves me and trusts me. I know that to honor God, I must learn to control myself. I have to learn to act as Jesus would act. He would never let other people make him lose his temper. I must learn to be like him. Life goes better when we try our best to be like Jesus."

Here is another journal entry from when I was 10 years old.

"Have you ever witnessed a geyser of blood squirting from your body similar to the water geysers squirting in Yellowstone National Park? I'm here to tell you it was one of the scariest times of my life.

"It was the early summer of 1980 and my older brother Colin and I were in the front yard doing our chores. My chore

46

at the time was sweeping our huge driveway while Colin was cleaning his fish tank, in which he kept snakes. Colin took pride in showing friends the large King Snake he had caught while on a hike.

"Do you know that saying, 'one boy, one brain; two boys, half a brain; and three boys, no brain at all'? Well, while Mom and Dad were in the house not looking, I would horse around and tease my older brother. Eventually coming to the end of his endurance, it was time for him to exercise some discipline on his psycho little brother, me.

"We started punching and kicking, eventually wrestling on the driveway. When we were finished with our match, I decided I was going to get the last kick in. So when he wasn't paying attention, I aimed a kick at his face. The kick was going smoothly until he caught my foot in mid-air. Unbalanced, I fell to the ground.

"Talk about being ticked off! I was in an uproar of anger. I wanted to get him back big time, so with no hesitation I walked to his snake tank and hit it so hard my hand went crashing through the glass. Reflexively, I yanked my hand out and naturally cut my wrist very deeply, all the way down to the main blood vein.

"I didn't know it was deep until a geyser of blood was squirting about a foot high off my wrist. My brother and I were amazed. I panicked like a chicken with its head cut off.

"I remember screaming and running for Mom. I ran inside the house, blood squirting all over the walls, looking for my mother. I found her, and she quickly got a towel and applied direct pressure. She was as scared as I was. I was screaming, thinking I was surely a goner.

"We got into the car, drove to the hospital, and demand-
ed medical attention right then and there. The doctor said I cut
my main artery by forcefully yanking my arm into the glass
that was still intact as I pulled it out of the snake tank.
It cut my flesh deeper.

"I will never forget being so scared, thinking that I was
going to die. I was sure I'd bleed to death. Later that summer I
paid the consequences for my behavior when our family went
camping at a lake. I had to sit out and watch everybody swim
while I tried not to get my cut infected. It was a long unevent-
ful summer. The open wound took all summer to heal, while
everybody else was playing. I was just thankful to be alive. I
learned a valuable lesson that year: there are consequences for
your actions, and sometimes you pay more dearly than at other
times."

Here is another example:

"Drills can be a weapon as well as a very useful tool. It
was a nice morning in the year of 1982 and I had nothing better to do than pester my older brother and his friend while they
fixed their car. My brother had told me to get way from them
before I got hurt. I took that as a challenge, and so started to
really bug him. When someone bugs you for awhile, they grow
impatient, and that's exactly what he did. He came after me,
but my quickness exceeded his.

"Huh…." I thought, "I am going to bug him again!"

His friend threatened to use the drill in his hand and drill
me to bits. Well, what did I do? I ran right towards him,

screaming "Drill me!"

"Sure enough, I ran right into the drill as it was turning, and it drilled right into my upper leg about a quarter of an inch. It hurt! What was I thinking, doing that? I had accepted the challenge of defeating my brother and his friend, and once again I paid the consequences for my actions."

MANY THANKS TO MY FOSTER PARENTS
FOR PUTTING UP WITH ME

I AM SO FORTUNATE TO HAVE HAD FOSTER PARENTS WHO NEVER GAVE UP ON ME. They had a motto they always used: "If you have a shoe, you need a mate." They believed in family. My foster parents were very special to me, although being the hell-raiser I was it wasn't always obvious. I DO CONSIDER THEM MY MOM AND DAD. THEY HAVE EARNED IT! I have an undying gratitude for what they did for me. They were both schoolteachers and devoted their time to helping me grow, both mentally and emotionally. Their love for children was expressed in the size of the family they had. When I joined, there were five children. Later on it became a family of nine, including their own kids and other long-term foster children.

They were extremely patient, with a loving but heavy hand, and they loved me unconditionally. But, man!—I was constantly testing the limits of that unconditional love. No doubt it was tested to the extreme. They had to put up with much that the average parents may not have to. They are saints. They have done their duty with love, and have paid the price to have me call them Mom and Dad. I was definitely a handful, and they had to endure far more than what was expected of them as foster parents. They were very tolerant. Ask yourself, would you have kept me as a foster kid after reading the following little stories?

Here are a few short stories about what they had to deal with. Some are very serious. I don't consider many of the events I'm going to tell about very funny. I don't take them lightly. This was serious stuff, and my bad choices often impacted others in negative ways. I am very sorry to the individuals who I hurt in the past. I am merely sharing with you a few examples of what I put my foster parents through. This will give you a feel for my personality and behavior at that time.

Here we go, this is some real stuff.

As a young boy I had a fascination with knives and guns. I would always fantasize about cutting people with a knife. From the normal person's point of view, I was a pretty twisted little boy. When I was about seven years old I found a razor blade, and started to carry it around in my pocket. One day when my neighborhood friend, about three years younger than I, would not do what I said, I took out my razor blade and threatened him. I wanted him to go down the hill on his Big-Wheel. Razor blade held out threateningly, I told him that if he didn't go down the hill on his Big-Wheel, I'd cut him.

Well he didn't go down the hill because he was scared to. It was a big hill. As I was yelling and swiping the air in front of him with the razor blade, he got very frightened. Trying to protect himself, he stretched his hands out to shield his body, and I proceeded to purposely cut his hand with the blade. It cut through the webbing of skin between the thumb and first finger. The cut went completely down to the bone. Blood was flowing everywhere. He ran screaming all the way home. I then went home and didn't tell anyone about the incident, wishing it would just go away. Soon after, the Dad next door called my Dad, and then all hell broke loose. They wanted to talk with me and my father when they returned from the emergency room.

When they finally got back and we went over to their house, my friend's Dad was so angry with me that he wanted to do the punishing. He wanted to give me a hard spanking. My Mom and Dad were extremely upset over me taking my stabbing fantasy out on a neighbor boy. I felt terrible too, and knew I was going to be in big-time trouble with the county and my social worker. This event pretty well cured me of my fascination with knives.

Thank goodness I never killed anyone. I ran into my neighborhood friend a couple years back at a motorcycle shop. We are now in our 30's, and he'd heard that my music was starting to get noticed. He told me if I ever make it big time, he's going to get his scar tattooed. He showed me the old scar and it was quite big. I wish it had never happened. I am so sorry for doing what I did, and I deeply thank him for forgiving me.

Onto a much different story; one not quite as violent.

Living on the farm, I had many opportunities to find insects and play with them. There was one insect in particular abundance, and there were always tons of them crawling around under boards and logs. These were pincher bugs. They are little bugs, about half an inch long, with big ugly pinchers.

There were dozens, if not hundreds or thousands of pincher colonies on the property. One day I had just finished the last of my Tic-Tac breath mints, and decided to use the empty container as an insect box. So I scooped up lots of pincher bugs, stuffing them in until the clear little box was almost full to capacity. The container was perfect for me, because I could just carry all the insects around in my pocket and they'd never get out. I was now like a walking insect aquarium.

My parents knew about my little insect collection. They didn't know, however, that I took the Tic-Tac container with me to school one day so I could show my classmates all my cool bugs. At recess I was hanging out with some friends, and a few of the girls were teasing me. I told them to stop but they wouldn't. It made me mad so I took out the Tic-Tac container, opened it up, and shook it wildly in the air in order to spray them with bugs. The pincher bugs were flying out of the container and into the girls' hair. I was so busted. Everything got chaotic from there, and I was called into the principal's office and suspended from school.

I got suspended a lot in elementary school, mostly for fighting. One of the crazier times at school was in the fourth grade, when I started a gang called the Hell's Angels Juniors. Every morning at the baseball field, my three friends and I would take black felt-tip pens and "tattoo" the words "Hell's Angels Juniors" on our upper arms so we could hide it from teachers and parents.

I don't know how I knew about Hell's Angels at that time, but I knew I wanted to belong to something big, and a bad, tough motorcycle gang seemed perfect for me. For the record, I am not a Hell's Angel.

I remember at that time there was a lot of trouble between what were called High Riders and Low Riders. I considered myself a High Rider. I got in lots of fights as a High Rider, and was suspended several times. While in fourth grade I got into a fight with a Low Rider and he knocked my tooth out. I was so mad. I'd been beaten up. We got him back later by scaring the crap out of him. He later became my friend for the rest of the school year. But the following year he went on to junior high and I was now a fifth grader. As a fifth grader I was now considered "King of the School," meaning that nobody would take me on in a fight or disrespect me. I had proven myself as a fighter and a force not to be messed with.

I had a system going on in elementary school. It was quite elaborate for a kid my age. When the bus would drop me off in front of school, I wouldn't go in and instead ran down the street, taking a side road over the hill to the candy shop. When I was done buying candy I would come back to school and be marked tardy. But I had my stash of candy in a brown paper bag, so I was happy.

I would also cut school during recess or the lunch hour just to get to the candy store. At recess I would have a friend in my gang distract the yard-duty supervisor at the tether-ball poles so a buddy of mine and I could slip out the back gate. We ran as fast as we could to make it to the candy store and back by the time the bell rang for class. We'd buy Jolly Rancher Stix and Now-and-Later candies for a nickel a piece, then sell them on the playground for a quarter. After a while, I no longer ditched to buy candy. Instead, I would recruit runners and they'd ditch recess to bring the candy stash back to me.

Soon my friend and I decided to take things a step further, so ditched lunch to go for a hamburger. The fast food place was pretty far away but we made it. On the way back, while we were walking up the hill, I saw my Dad's orange VW Bug coming up behind us. I could have seen that bright orange car coming from a mile away. I was freaking out. I told my friend that I just saw my Dad's car, and urged him to remain calm. I had to look calm, cool and collected in front of my friend, so I just said to keep going up the hill and look straight ahead.

Whatever he did, he was not to look at the cars going by. The orange VW went by up the hill. 'Whew…I'm safe,' I thought. But my Dad must have seen us in the rear-view mirror, because he stopped his car right then and there. I told my friend to run, but he didn't. I knew I'd been caught. My Dad waited for us to walk by the car. He asked what we were doing out of school. I told him we were hungry, so we left. We got into the car. He drove us back to school and brought us to the principal's office. I remember getting a lot of detentions because of that. Thanks for ratting us out, Dad!

Another fun adventure that got me into a lot of trouble was a time when my Dad was at the police station taking care of a ticket.

I must have been around twelve years old. He had me wait in the truck while he took care of the issue. After waiting a while, I was beginning to get bored, so I got out of the truck and saw a few nails on the floorboard. I grabbed them and put them in my pocket. I looked around the parking lot at all the cars. I decided that I wanted to have a little fun, so I walked around looking for intriguing vehicles and let the air out of their tires. I used the tip of the nail to push in the tire valve, letting the air out. It was fun because I got to sneak around. I was popping my head out from behind one of the cars when I saw the big prize, a bunch of police cars parked in a gated lot. The gate happened to be open. I took the chance and crept right through it.

I felt like a highly trained soldier, making myself invisible. I hid behind one of the police cruisers and took a glance around the premises to see if there was anybody around. It was clear, so I proceeded to let the air out of the tires. I also set some nails up in front of the tires so that when the police officer drove out he or she would roll over them and get their tires punctured. I did this to a few cars when all of a sudden I saw policemen coming out the rear door of the building, running towards me. I tried to hide, but it was too late. They grabbed me and brought me inside. They sat me down in an office and held me there. I told them I was here with my Dad. I asked one of the policeman, "How did you catch me?" He said there were cameras stationed all over the building. They notified my Dad and he came to get me. I was in big trouble and my Dad was terribly embarrassed.

The police let me go with a strong warning. My Dad, on the other hand, put me to a lot of hard work on the farm and placed me on "restriction." I guess that was better than juvenile hall.

One of my favorite idiotic times occurred when I was returning to school from an early morning church event. A senior in high school let my friends and me catch a ride with him back to school. What he didn't know was that I was thinking very mischievous thoughts, and had plans to give him a good scare. My friends and I were sitting in the back seats of his big van. There were side windows, but they only opened up a little. Just enough to throw jumping jacks out of. Jumping jacks are as big as firecrackers, but when ignited they jump and spin, letting off sparks and a loud crackling sound. I had a ton of these things. I would light the jumping jacks and throw them out the window at people walking or jogging on the streets. The driver didn't notice a thing. When we got to school, we thanked him for the ride. But before we left I opened up the front passenger door, lit two jumping jacks and threw them at him. He was in shock! My friends were in shock! I wanted to show my friends that I wasn't scared of doing anything. They landed on him but eventually fell down at his feet by the pedals. They were spinning and jumping around the gas and brake pedals. He was kicking his feet and screaming in a panic while I was laughing and getting a big kick out of it. My friends were totally scared for me then.

After the fireworks had stopped he was so mad that he got out of the van and came over to give me a hard punch in the chest. He was a senior in high school and I was a freshman—a big difference in age and size. I took the punch like a man. He was yelling at me and said he was going to tell my Mom and Dad.

Now I was the one who was scared! I didn't show it though. I left with my friends and went to class, but I couldn't help thinking how busted I was going to be when I got home. I was really worried. As the day went by, I happened to see the senior and went up to him while nobody was looking and told him how sorry I was and to please not tell my parents. He told me he'd think about it. He could tell how scared I was. I was no longer that bulletproof little freshman he'd seen earlier that morning. He now saw the vulnerable and frightened freshman. He made me suffer for the rest of the day. I went home without knowing whether he'd told my parents what had happened.

They didn't bring it up that night. I saw him again at school the next day and he promised not to tell my parents. I told him, "Thank you so much for letting me live another day." I was never mean to that guy again.

Now what do you think of when you think of a Boy Scout? Do you think of good little boys who want to help out others and are always prepared? Well that wasn't me when I was a Scout. I joined the Boy Scouts because it was mandatory in my family. I don't regret it. It was a lot of fun. But I didn't live up to the example that Boy Scouts are supposed to portray. Call me a Wild Scout hanging out with a bunch of boys. I enjoyed all the camping and special activities, but I wasn't too fond of participating in the community service projects.

At least I can claim to have never had a problem with cheating or dishonesty. That was one very important thing I had going, and that I am still proud of. I am happy that honesty was a major part of my character, but I did have other problems. I would not respect authority or the older Boy Scouts. At Scout Camp, I got into countless fights with a few of the older members. I definitely pushed the limits. I was not considered a leader, nor was I considered a particular good example to the rest of the troop. I had a potty mouth, was constantly instigating trouble, and refused to do things any way but my own. I always wanted to get attention, even if it was the wrong type of attention.

My parents had a rule in our family which had it that boys could not get their driver's license until they had earned the rank of an Eagle Scout, the highest possible in Boy Scouts. This was a big task for me. I had to do a lot of extra community service, earn merit badges, and set a good example for the other kids. At sixteen, when all the other boys got their Eagle, I was still a long way from getting mine. I decided to wait it out and see if my parents wouldn't cave in and tell me to just go ahead and get my license. But they were adamant and their minds couldn't be changed. By the time I turned seventeen, I could see that they were dead serious about me earning my Eagle. All of my friends had their licenses, and for transportation I always had to bum a ride off them.

But as I was slowly approaching my eighteenth birthday, the cut-off age for getting an Eagle, I started to hustle. I definitely wanted a license by my senior year.

I worked hard and did my big Eagle project, and it seemed like I had made it just in time. But the hardest part of getting the

Eagle is not necessarily earning the badges and doing the projects, it's passing the Eagle Board of Review.It was a panel of four or more Scout leaders, and you had to stand before them to be interviewed. They wanted to know why you thought you deserved to be awarded the highest rank in Boy Scouts. I thought I had secured my badge by completing my Eagle Project, but that was far from the case. While the leaders interviewed me, they brought up all the bad things I'd ever done as a Scout, and grilled me with questions. It felt like an interrogation more than an interview. Why did I do all those things? They asked why I hadn't been able to set a good example of Boy Scout virtues. I told them I didn't know. I had no answers for my scouting behavior. It just was what it was. I made no excuses, but neither did accept responsibility.

After they were done asking me their series of questions, they asked me wait outside in the hall while they discussed my worthiness to obtain the Eagle. After waiting for a long time on pins and needles, I started to get worried about what might happen. They had the power to deny me my Eagle Scout ranking, and that meant I wouldn't be getting my driver's license. If I didn't have my license, I wouldn't be cool for my entire senior year. As I entered the room, they all looked at me with somber faces. I knew right away something was wrong. They informed me that I hadn't set a good enough example for scouting, and they were not passing me through the Eagle Board of Review.   But they did decide to postpone their final decision, which bought me a few weeks. At the end of that time, I could come back and give them a more convincing reason as to why I should be an Eagle Scout. Basically they wanted me to beg them for it. I despised the fact that they had the power and authority to stop me from getting my license. But I thanked them for the chance to return and argue my case.

That was a long couple of weeks, and embarrassing for my Mom and Dad. They were both very big supporters of scouting, especially since my two older brothers were certified Eagle Scouts. I couldn't believe I'd been denied.

For all my years of scouting, this was what it had come down to. I thought for the next couple weeks about how scouting had affected me and how it had played a positive role in my life. When I went back to stand before the Review, I thanked them again for the opportunity, and the leniency they displayed in giving me a second chance. I then turned on my charm and told them how much scouting had helped me grow. I apologized for all my erratic behavior and that I felt sad about not having applied myself in a better manner. I told them I worked hard for my Eagle Scout, and had set a good example for my troop on the Eagle Project. I said I had evolved as a Scout, and that holding me accountable for my past behavior would be short-sighted. I had grown a lot in the past year, and Scouts was all about personal growth and turning into a man.
I made them feel comfortable about letting me pass. I had convinced them that I would now take scouting seriously, and pass on the spirit of personal growth to others.

They passed me and I was ecstatic! I felt like I had started to evolve into a man, and now had to live up to the responsibility of being an Eagle. I learned the hard way, but the Eagle is a bird who is a leader and never flies in a flock. They are the true noble birds that soar above all others. I was now considered one of them. I no longer wanted to be considered a pigeon. I was an Eagle! And even to this day, I try to live up to the promise I made. That I would be an example of what an Eagle does. I take pride in the fact that I did earn it, working hard and suffering for my past actions. I'm grateful that they gave me a second chance to prove myself.

Here is an incident in which I almost got shot.

In high school, I would sometimes affiliate myself with other fighters. They had told me one Friday at school that that night they were going to fight another crew from another school. The fight was to take place at this club off the boulevard we used to cruise our cars on. That night we all met in the parking lot. There was a lot of people hanging out. Our crew was waiting until the other school's crew showed up. In the meantime, we were acting crazy and loud. We saw another crew gathering, a gang who didn't like our high school. They started giving us dirty looks, then came up to us yelling and threatening. It turned into a huge brawl. Everyone was swinging.

Others were joining them and we had to back up, eventually retreating. I ran across the street to wait the rumble out, but there were a bunch of people following me. The fight had spilled out into the street by now. People were running everywhere. All of a sudden I heard gun shots, and fear started to pump through my veins. My heart was beating out of my chest, and I was trying not to get caught up in the crossfire. Everyone was running and scrambling around like crazy when another gunshot went off. The bullet from that gunshot hit the garbage dumpster right behind me. I thought I was going to be killed. I just ran in a panic down the street as fast as I could when I saw my friend drive by in his truck yelling, "Derek get in!" I didn't even hesitate, jumping into the back of the truck and getting face down as we went tearing down the highway.

I was definitely a rebellious kid, but not by doing drugs or drinking alcohol. I never got into experimenting with drugs, and in fact I've never tried them. I don't know what it's like to be high, at least not any higher than my crazy personality already made me feel. In school, I would never apply myself. I always preferred to be the class clown or the fighter.
I was never interested in getting good grades, nor was I into letting authority figures tell me what to do. I was bored a lot. I was a musician and yet I got straight D's in symphonic band class. Man, if my band teacher could only see me now. I have accomplished a lot musically. I just believe that the classroom environment was not well-suited to my brand of self-expression.

I almost didn't graduate high school, due to a particular incident. It was the spring semester, and as usual I was just doing my own thing. I was eighteen most of my senior year, and technically an adult. This meant I could write my own notes to get out of class. I'd normally go to the beach and surf. This was fun, but I don't recommend it—kids, stay in school! One day I was hanging out in English class and, as usual, making rude comments just to get a few laughs. My teacher said to me, "You shouldn't talk like that. You're a Christian and go to those early morning Bible studies." I told her I could do whatever I wanted. She was actually a very nice woman, but because of my immaturity I had no respect for her. I was not afraid to tell her off in front of the whole class.

I verbally exploded on her, like I was the one in charge of class. I called her some very profanity-laced names. I'll just let you imagine what they were. She told me to get out of the class, but I refused, so she called the assistant principal to come and get me. I took my bag and got out of there before the assistant principal came. I ran. I was gone. Later that day, I showed up at the assistant principal's office and sat down to tell her I'd been kicked out of the class. She already knew, of course, and informed me that the teacher never wanted me back in her class again, on account of my language and disrespect. They decided they were going to expel me from school. I had to call my Mom from the assistant principal's office and tell her what happened. I let her know that I was no longer allowed to be in school. I went home, very embarrassed and very much in trouble. My parents got involved and were able to save me from being completely expelled. I ended up only expelled from English class, and I now had to take English in the assistant principal's waiting room every day. If I didn't show up and do my work I'd be expelled completely.

This happened a couple months prior to graduation, and I'd heard from my counselor that I wasn't on track to graduate. This was unbelievable to me. I couldn't fathom that I was going to flunk high school. She said the only way to make sure I graduated was to bring my grades up within a month. Despite the warning, I didn't try any harder. Then when all of my friends were ordering their special graduation announcement cards; ordering their caps, gowns, and tassels; and planning their graduation parties, I was totally bummed and felt like a failure.

I didn't even bring the order sheet home to my parent's because I knew I wasn't going to be getting my diploma. It was embarrassing having to tell my friends that I wouldn't be walking the graduation stage with them. I was ashamed. I remembered how I'd been kicked out of my kindergarten class, and now here I was basically getting kicked out of high school. I decided at that point, at the eleventh hour, to get serious and apply myself. If I could at least get some passing grades I could walk the stage with my classmates.

Over the next month I was doing all of my homework and working hard, but I didn't know for sure if this effort would be enough to earn the required grades. I worked and worked without having any idea of what the end result might be.

Then about a week before graduation, my counselor called me into her office and told me I would be able to graduate. I had done what was barely sufficient to make it. I was ecstatic and overjoyed. I could not believe it! This was the best news I'd heard in a long time. I told all of my friends and family, and they were totally excited. The next mission was to get a tassel, cap and gown. So I borrowed my friend's extra tassel, which he had hanging from his car mirror. I borrowed my foster brother's cap and gown, which he still had from his graduation a couple of years before mine. It was torn up from partying the day of his graduation. Adding to its shabbiness was the fact that my brother was about five foot, ten inches, but I was six foot, five inches. The gown was way too short and the cap barely fit my big head. But it worked. I walked that stage with profound gratitude and a happy sense of accomplishment. I had managed to graduate with a 1.83 GPA. Talk about cutting it close.

I could go on and on about the many times I got into trouble for yelling profanities at my parents or getting into fights with teachers, church leaders, and other adults. But that would be a book in itself. All that's left to say is that I am eternally grateful to my foster Mom and Dad for never giving up hope on me. They never changed the locks on the front door or told the social worker to take me away. They serve as great examples of love and patience, enduring as they did the hard times which inevitably come when raising a messed up little kid. They didn't have to keep me. I wasn't adopted, so they could have given up on me at any time. But instead they chose to never give up on me, even when I gave them hell. They always shot back with a love that came from deep within their hearts, proving that love has the power to overcome the negative in any situation. Thank you so much Mom and Dad!

The Worth Of A Soul

The following poem is my all-time favorite. As you read it, try visualizing all the little children and teenagers who don't have a home or are in foster care. There is a reason why they don't have a home. It is their parents' fault! I believe it all comes down to the parents. Parents are responsible for shaping their kid's life. Period! The parents are selfish, possibly addicted to drugs or alcohol, and often physically and mentally abusing their children. Or maybe they just didn't want the child and so gave him or her up, which in any case boils down to selfishness. This mindset puts pleasure before love, inflicts pain before bestowing affection. These parents have given up on the only thing that matters, love. They've found a way to justify giving up. Maybe their parents did the same thing to them and they are carrying out the cycle once more.

End The Cycle!

When parents give up on these innocent children, children often give up too. The child gives up on themselves, has low self-esteem, lacks confidence and trust, and is all too commonly afraid of giving love unconditionally, burdened as he or she is with questions concerning their own self-worth. I know, I have been there!

This poem puts everything into perspective. I love it.

"The Touch of the Master's Hand"

Twas battered and scarred and the auctioneer, thought it
scarcely worth his while, to waste much time on the old violin,
but he held it up with a smile:

"What am I bidden, good folks." He cried,
"Who'll start the bidding for me?"
"A dollar, a dollar; then two, only two?
Two dollars, and who'll make it three?
Three dollars once, three dollars twice.
Going for three...." But no,
From the room far back, a grey haired man came forward and
picked up the bow.
Then, wiping the dust from the old violin, and tightening all
the loose strings,
He played a melody pure and sweet as the caroling angels
sing.
The music ceased, and the auctioneer with a voice that was
quiet and low,
Said "What am I bid for the old violin?" and he held it up with
the bow.
"A thousand dollars, and who'll make it two?
Two thousand and who'll make it three?
Three thousand once, three thousand twice and going and
gone. "Said he"

The people cheered, but some of them cried,
"We don't quite understand…
What changed its worth."
Swift came the reply;
"THE TOUCH OF THE MASTERS HAND."

"Now many a man with his life out of tune,
Battered and scarred with sin,
Is auctioned cheap to the thoughtless crowd,
Much like the old violin.
A mess of pottage, a glass of wine,
A game….and he travels on,
He is going once, and going twice,
He's going and almost "gone".
But the Master comes, and the foolish crowd,
Never can quite understand,
The Worth of a SOUL and the change that is wrought,
BY THE TOUCH OF THE MASTER'S HAND."

Written by Myra Brooks Welch

Awesome, isn't it?

It reminds us how valuable we really are, and how we sometimes sell ourselves short or let others determine our self-worth. If we let others determine who we are, and then don't live up to those false standards or expectations, we become depressed, falling into a slump which drains the life from us. People are the most valuable thing on this Earth. It's not your house, your car or how much money you have in your savings.

The worth of a soul cannot be determined by material possessions. Lets face it, you can't have a U-Haul trailer on the back
of your hearse when you are about to meet your maker. Some
of the happiest people I know are far from being rich. We are
the only ones capable of directing our lives toward enriching
goals. There will never be another person like you to walk this
Earth. Remember your uniqueness!

A LITTLE BOY'S NIGHTMARE

I have had a recurring nightmare since I was a little kid. It has caused me great confusion, as it deals with the possibility that God never loved me. This nightmare still haunts me, even in my adulthood. I've always wondered whether there was some truth to this nightmare. If not, why have I kept having it for all these years?

I am a little kid, about five years old, running through a field of yellow grass. A man is chasing me. The sun is going down and darkness quickly approaching. I can't see who the man is, but he is angry with me and I am very scared. As I run, I keep looking over my shoulder to see if he is gaining ground on me. I can feel my heart beating so strongly in my chest. It is getting darker.

Over a rolling hill, I see a church with a large steeple and huge stained-glass windows. I run to it. I am very small in comparison to the church. I pull the enormous double-doors open and run inside. There is a loud bang behind me as the doors close. The church is dark, lit only by the weak flame of a few candles. The man is still chasing me. I can hear him screaming outside, so I run around the church trying to find a hiding place. The many grim statues are scary. They're staring at me, as are the faces in the stained-glass. The walls and floors arc dark grey, and seem to be made of stone and cold cement. The air is chilly. It is not a warm or comforting place. I do not feel protected. I do not feel safe. I haven't found a hiding place. I continue to run. The building is so very large.

I run down to the end of a long hallway and try to open the set of doors there. They are locked. The man chasing me is now inside the church. I can hear him screaming. Suddenly, in a very low, deep, and evil voice he calls me by my name. I do not recognize his voice. I have never heard anger like the anger I hear in his voice, nor have I ever been this scared. My heart is pounding intensely.

I really believe I am going to die. I hide behind a large statue in the corner and see a dark figure opening the doors with ease, as if they were opened by some demonic power. The sound of the doors crashing open echoes through my ears. My frightened breath is coming in gasps, and I fear the man can hear me taking in air. I wonder if this will be the final moments of my life.

I sneak out from behind the statue, going down the hallway and into a big room with lots of pews. I hide behind one of them, but it doesn't feel safe. It seems as if all the many statues in the walls are staring at me in order to give away my hiding place. It's as if they are conspiring with this man; are on the same side. I notice that all the statues have wings, as does the man in the shadows. I can see the silhouettes of his wings as he walks around in the dark. As I lay there sweating profusely in the darkness, my heart nearly beating out of my chest, I know that my life depends on my being silent.

And then, with no resolution, I wake up with the vague and disturbing feeling of being unsafe, that nobody will come to my rescue, that there is nobody protecting me.

Having analyzed this dream time and again throughout my life, I have come to the conclusion that there is something either with Church or God that doesn't sit right with me. I feel no love or protection. I do pray everyday and read the Bible. I do all the things my foster family and church has taught me to do, but feel I am still unable to enjoy intimate, meaningful communication with God. I have felt alone, in the spiritual sense, for so many years. I love the "Footprints in the Sand" poem, but I do not believe its message pertains to my own life. If I were to accept that message, I would then have to believe that Jesus carried me throughout my life. But I believe that where I am in life is solely due to free will and the choices I've made while exercising that will. If I hadn't made certain choices, I would be in a very different place in life.

LOST IN RELIGEON

I feel that I will likely be judged by my religious friends, family, and churches for the words I am about to write. I may disappoint them with how truthful I'm being. But I feel the only way for me to grow is by being completely honest about myself and my limited religious beliefs. My intent is to be completely real regarding my faith. I have to be honest so that my words can help other's who may think as I do. I am not here to be politically correct or water my feelings down. This is the truth that I must answer to every night when the lights go out and I am alone with my conscience. I have been involved in religion most of my life and have taken all the necessary steps in order to build my religious faith but yet I have not felt it. I have been told that if you go through the motions and make a daily habit of submitting myself to my religious faith, that it will grow. I am sad to say that it has not really grown, in some instances it has grown more mind-numbing and the pressure of trying to build my religious testimony has mentally wiped me out. I have faith in God, but not sure if I have faith in organized religion.

I have secretly questioned my religious faith in the past, but realize that now as an adult I don't have to worry about disappointing my parents, friends and church leaders. If they love me unconditionally, they will understand my feelings.

I wonder if they sometimes secretly doubt their faith and doubt their beliefs. I don't want it to be a secret, I want to know that they are not as perfect as they portray themselves to be and that they sometimes do waver in their faith.

I want to know if they struggle with those similar feelings like me. It has been stated that our life will change for the better when we accept Christ, that may be true but it also may lead to a life that is tainted with fakeness and self despair.

This is caused by trying to live up to the unrealistic expectations of trying to perfect ourselves when our internal true self is struggling because we are not truly happy. We mask our unhappiness by saying we are a happy Christian. I believe that our life will only change when we accept our internal true self. I am puzzled by self proclaimed happy Christians who speak with a smile but emit a vibe of ugly bitterness and unhappiness. They can't hide behind the mask with me. In order to come across as a true and genuinely happy person, I believe the next steps are to be followed. We must first strip off all of the armor of our ego, our painful baggage and the battle wounds of the past and accept who we really are at our core. Only you know the "real" you. We must first love ourselves and therefore it will emit a vibe of happiness and love without any effort because the mask of fakeness will have disappeared.

How does one really know the absolute and physical truth of God or God's love? Sure, I've heard all the stories in the Bible and other religious books, but these writings could be the word of God or just as easily be considered folklore, stories and examples handed down. I just don't know what to think about it but I believe that it definitely does more good than bad and I find those that live the Bible principles have a happier life. I know that the Bible teaches great principles of how to live life in a more peaceful state of mind. It teaches us how to forgive, not to judge and to love and turn the other cheek. It tells the wondrous miracles of Jesus and the love he had for mankind. The Bible shows that He was a great example for others and how much he sacrificed and yet still loved all. I would love to feel his love without a middle man brokering his love to me. I read the bible almost every day with my family because it sets forth great guidelines to live a righteous life and gives examples of choosing the right. It also divulges the consequences for those that made bad choices. Even though my faith is limited, I still enjoy learning the lessons of the Bible.

I often feel like Neo in the hit movie *The Matrix*, always searching for the mysterious "force behind reality," which in my case is God. Once in a while, I question whether God is really out there, and just rely on what everyone else says they feel about Him; their claims that they are certain their prayers have been answered. This keeps my faith going, and keeps the hope alive that one day He will answer my own prayers.

For most of my life, I've been searching and praying every day, but it usually feels like I'm praying to the wind because I've never felt that God has answered me. I have acted earnestly, and believed faith would come by participating in spiritual practices. And yet, my faith hasn't seemed to grow or even take root.

I have always struggled with the suffering of the innocent. I can only imagine the faith a mother has when her child is diagnosed with cancer and has only a few months to live. She is probably praying with utter sincerity and devotion to God, asking that He not take her child away, yet often the child passes on.

Faith arises from particular situations, and is the method whereby a person seeks comfort during times of need and suffering. I also feel for the starving children throughout the world, when they pray for food and food doesn't come. I think we all pray for the needy at times in hopes that God will show His mercy on those who suffer. When the mercy doesn't come, the value of faith is questioned.

Life is confusing and I don't always know what to believe. There are only a select few who can enjoy unwavering faith. They never question anything. It is like they have a knowledge others do not. I believe some people are directly connected to God, and it is beautiful to see this connection. But I am not one of those people. I would like to have that unwavering faith. Anyone who has suffered or gone through bad experiences either strengthens their faith or lets it fade away. I continually try to strengthen it day by day. But just because I don't have this unwavering faith doesn't mean that I don't believe in God or that I am not a Christian. I am always going through the process of questioning my faith, and I will never give up trying to find it.

I was the kind of person content to go through all the religious motions, but the motions didn't seem to inspire any true spiritual feelings. Sure, it was reverent, but realistically I was just trying to appear Godly. I'm sure every religion has great intentions, but it seems to me that we as a religious culture sometimes become too fanatic, and get off track when trying to decipher what God wants from us in this day and age. I have no intention of trying to sway or critique anybody's deeply held beliefs. I honestly applaud those who have faith. I can only hope that someday my faith will be as strong as the faith of my readers, friends, family, and churches.

But if those of strong religious conviction feel just in judging me, I can only say that I sincerely hope to never turn out like them. I don't ever want to have the kind of limiting faith that divides the "saved" from the "unsaved," or has it that one person is better than another solely on account of the beliefs they hold or do not hold.

While a lot my friends and family can give inspiring testimonies about God and how He has answered their prayers, I myself feel nothing. I have carried the burden of feeling unloved by God my entire life. I do feel blessed, only not from a religious perspective. Rather, blessed as a person who appreciates happiness and loves existence. I believe there is a God, and this God created this world, the universe, galaxies, every living person, animals, and organisms. But when I consider the billions of people and the great marvels of this world, all created by God, I feel so small and insignificant in relation to Him that it bars me from feeling a connection with Him. I do have a very strong testimony of inspiration.
I have felt inspired to write songs, write this book, to have a

family and other numerous examples. I feel I am open to inspiration but it doesn't come in a religious or faith building way. It comes through intuition and openness of mind. My inspirational moments are the closest I have ever been to God. I give him the credit of putting those thoughts in my mind. I then take action on them. Others have felt close to God in other ways, I yearn for that connection of Gods Spirit.

Despite not feeling a powerful connection with God, I can say with confidence it was a heavenly blessing that I ended up in a great foster home with a great family. But why did God allow me and so many others to be born into such stunningly dysfunctional environments? Why did I have to suffer more than most kids? My foster family introduced religious structure into my life. **There are good things about church organizations and there are not-so-good things.** Since we always hear about the good church offers, I thought I might elaborate on some of the bad. As a teenager I found church to be fun, but it wasn't always about spirituality. Many of the youth would be disrespectful to others, smoke weed, drink alcohol, have sex and get pregnant. We were definitely not being great examples of our faith or acting Christ like. It didn't matter whether we were going to church or not. We indulged in vice because we could.

Looking back, church was actually a breeding ground for rebelliousness. There was so much emphasis on what not to do that these behaviors became great temptations.

I had many good times at church dances and other events.

But as a parent, I believe that I shouldn't turn a blind and blissfully ignorant eye to religious youth programs, believing them to be safe simply because they're church-related. There are lots of rebellious teenagers who aren't going to church to become a better person, and instead go for the social life or because their parents are forcing them to. The parents may think that church can fix their kid, without realizing that their child may be tempting the good little church kids into doing wrong. Just because a person participates in church activities doesn't automatically make them a Godly or Christ-like person. Be watchful, rebels need an audience.

There is an overwhelming number of people who act like they are perfect, but it's not hard to spot the fakeness hiding behind their masks of perfection. This is the hypocritical "holier than thou" mentality. I cannot stand hanging out with somebody who isn't "real." I'm all for trying to perfect ourselves, but just be you and be true. Who cares if you fall? If there are truly religious people around you, they will try to help pick you up and put you back on your feet.

There is the term "service with a smile," but I believe it should be SERVICE WITH YOUR HEART. Smiles can be easily faked. Like attracts like, so if you have a holier-than-thou persona and consider yourself superior to others, this is the kind of crowd you're going to associate with. But if you are a genuine and real person striving to improve yourself, you know you have faults and aren't a perfect human being.
I have seen many people in churches who have become full of themselves. Their belief that their truth is the only way to

Heaven makes them egotistical. As they become consumed with their "truth," they turn cliquish, judging and looking down on others who are equally convinced of their own personal truths. They do the very thing which Jesus said not to do: "Judge not, lest ye be judged." Being Christ-like does not of necessity make you better than the homeless man addicted to alcohol.

Jesus forgave all men, and preached that the greatest Master is also the greatest Servant. I believe one has to work extremely hard at becoming a better person. It doesn't come easy, and takes more than the standard displays of religious faith. Many churches profess that their way is the only way to Heaven. So many people act as "salvation brokers," claiming that they alone know the will of God and what is right for you. But they don't know what's right for me, I know what's right for me. I am open to listening, but as a man I must interpret what they're saying in my own "God given" common sense way. In the end it all comes down to whether I am a follower or a leader. Leaders always need followers, and being a follower is a lot easier than being a leader. There is nothing wrong with being a follower if you are given all the facts and know exactly what you are in for.

Be careful of leaders that have all the answers, because no one has all the answers. They have their personal interpretations, but those interpretations are worthless opinions that they are trying to sell to your belief system. That is the truth! Do not allow your mental hard drive to get programmed in the name of religion without first questioning it. Do not follow just because it is comfortable for you to follow or to be a part of something to follow. You are better than that. If we had someone that had all the answers and could foresee our destiny, then the 9/11 tragedy would have been avoided or all wars and the suffering all around the world cease to exist. Do not let a persons smooth talking and theatrics cancel out the brain that God has given you to think and question for yourself. The Bible teaches us to question all things. In 1st Thessalonians 5:21 it states "Prove all things; hold fast that which is good." To prove something, you must first question it. Questions bring about facts and the proof is therefore shown.

I don't just do something because a supposedly God-Inspired person tells me it's what God wants me to do. I'm an independent thinker and can use my own mind, the mind that God Himself has given me. I can use what is called "God-given common sense." Don't fall into the trap of being manipulated or made to feel guilty. Manipulation through guilt is a powerful man-made tool that religious leaders often use against people in order to persuade them to do what they want. It's all about having power over others.

I trust nobody regarding their opinions on the truth. The only way we can know what truth is if it comes straight from God, and if He is inclined to give us the truth, then we know it's real. When flesh and blood men and women put themselves between God and His followers, you can be sure there is a hidden agenda. Church leaders should concern themselves only with love, not judgment. They are human beings too.

Many church leaders have given into terrible temptations. This would not be the case if these people were truly following God, because if God is anything, He is pure love.

Churches should realize that their organization shouldn't be so much about money. They say "Give tithes in the name of God," or, "God's church needs more money!" What it all boils down to is "Pay, and ye shall be blessed." This is manipulative rhetoric. Do you really think God needs your money? He doesn't; man does. I don't doubt that there are some serious offenses being committed with the money people give. How much money is enough? Is it a race to see which church is the richest? Churches should focus on the religious basics of changing people's lives for the better in the name of God!!! Save for the special case of relieving poverty, it doesn't take any money to change a person's life. All it takes is an open ear and time.

In the Bible it is stated quite simply, "And though I have the gift of prophecy, and understand all mysteries and all knowledge, and though I have all faith, so that I could remove mountains, but have not love, I am nothing. And though I bestow all my goods to feed the poor, and though I give my body to be burned, but have not love, it profits me nothing. Love suffers long and is kind; love does not envy; love does not parade itself, is not puffed up. Love does not behave rudely, does not seek its own, is not provoked, and thinks no evil. Love does not rejoice in iniquity, but rejoices in the truth. Love bears all things, believes all things, hopes all things, endures all things.
    - *1 Corinthians 13 NKJV*

There are so many people who aim to make faith a confusing matter, expressing their own biases, and then manipulating others through fear and guilt into believing that their way is the proclaimed way to Heaven. Everyone neurotically defends their own way to Heaven. Religion can be used to justify any act, whether hateful or loving, and there are fanatics everywhere committing unforgivable acts in the name of their God. In the film, *Kingdom of Heaven*, there was a line of dialogue that to me rang very true: ***"I put no stock in religion. By the word of religion, I've seen the lunacy of fanatics of every denomination be called the Will of God. Holiness is in right actions and courage. What God desires is a good heart and a good mind."***

The truth is that nobody knows the truth. We listen to others opinions and interpretations and sometimes label them as truth, but if you get down to the nuts and bolts of it, the truth may not be the truth. Yes, I have had moments of what I would call spiritual peace, and moments of spiritual reverence, but I don't know what to believe. Sure we have the Bible, but it has been translated so many times, and typically only scholars read it in the original Hebrew and Greek. I believe that one word being mistranslated, or an original term improperly understood, leads to sects interpreting passages or ideas in an incorrect way, perhaps taking as literal fact what was meant to be metaphorical. Interpretations might even be based on typographical errors. We have to trust that the translator translating the Bible is making absolutely no mistakes. I for one don't believe everything I read. It is good to be an independent thinker and question everything.

So how can I search for a truth that is untainted by a man's errors and what may be a hidden agenda? I pray for truth, but I've never heard the "still, small voice" that provides a convincing answer. Nor have I heard the thundering voice of God speaking to me. I can wish and hope for things unseen, but I have never known anyone who has come back from the other side to tell me their way is the only way and the only truth. Churches can build beautiful buildings and enjoy big congregations. They can have movies, music, and all the things that together create an image of perfect religious reverence. They can package it all up and call it the word of God, claiming that the Holy Spirit guides all their actions. They may even say that their church is better than others churches, or that their message is truer than the message of other churches. But in the end, it's all based on something unseen.

I see congregations taking a church leader at his word—a man's word—never questioning how this man interprets God's will. But I believe religion is man's interpretation, and doesn't necessarily reflect the will of God.

Even with all the suffering in the world, church leaders still say "Ask and ye shall receive." I have come to realize that I can no longer entertain this "wish upon a star" frame of mind. It encourages spiritual weakness, and puts rescue outside of our own hands and beyond our control. My understanding of free will leads me to conclude that God does not intervene in our lives, and does not grant wishes. If it were otherwise, all the wishes of all the people suffering would be granted, and this appears to not be the case. If God does intervene but hasn't been willing to do so in these cases, that would imply He is playing favorites. I am no more important than the starving children of the world. Why would he answer my prayers, while theirs go ignored? The plain and simple fact is that if you want something done, you have to do it yourself. I have always lived according to this belief, and have enjoyed great success. What I sow, I reap. The responsibility is all mine. Free will, as I understand it, is a gift that empowers us and calls us to action.

There seems to be a lot of talk these days about predestination. If I accepted this creed, I would have to believe my life was already planned out in detail according to God's grand design. But I believe in free will. It's all about taking responsibility for the choices that will determine our destiny. I cannot buy into the idea that some master puppeteer in the sky is controlling my life. We must become what we want through our self-willed actions. In the past, I often deferred to people who were all-too willing to tell me what God wanted of me. I no longer allow them to do so. I cut out the middle man, and seek God directly. Even if I still haven't had the communication with God that I've sought for so long, it feels good to be an independent thinker, and to shrug off the yoke which organized religion has tried to throw around my neck.

More than simply taking beliefs at face value, I believe what is required is that we have faith in the unknown. Faith enables us to make manifest our dreams and lead us to our ultimate destination.

Our faith will fail us at times, but we have to regain it. It's no different than getting back on the horse to ride after a fall. Strength comes from the falls, and our character shows by what we do afterward.

It's easy for some to attribute all their successes to God. But in the darkness and silence that sometimes overcomes me, when I must give an honest assessment of my life and answer to my conscience, I don't always share with others the conviction that God is responsible for our victories in life. Think of the boxer who has just won an amazing fight and then gives God the credit for his win. I personally believe it wasn't God who helped him beat up his opponent. Did God come down and tell the boxer when and where to punch?
It would be great to have an invisible friend who told us how to win at everything all the time, but it's not reality. The boxer himself, along with his trainers, are to credit for the victory.

I can't say that all of my Mom's and Dad's lectures or punishments shaped me into the person I am today. I might say the same about my church's continual interviews and pressure-tactics, which they used to make me feel guilty about every bad thing I'd ever done. To be honest, I ignored a lot of it. It felt like micro-management of my spirituality. All of that just made me rebel more. So parents, my advice is don't let church raise your child. You yourself should take the time and listen to your kids. If they've messed up according to your standards, just love them and try to make them feel good about making good choices. Unless they've broken the laws of this land, there should be no need to have a third party punish them. These are your children, not the church's. I am all about building a person up, not tearing them down to the point where they are vulnerable to depression, insecurities, low self-esteem and lack of self-confidence. This is not Godly.

What did Jesus do when others were judging a prostitute? He told them not to judge, and told the lady to go and sin no more. Did he punish her and make her feel like a piece of garbage? No! How beautiful is that! It's all about building a person up and lovingly encouraging them to try better the next time. I don't agree with either a layman or a man of the cloth acting as God's judge and making somebody feel bad about the choices they've made. A church leader is just a man with sins that he hides from the world.

There is no perfect man on this Earth. If somebody claims to be perfect they are lying, and if they are lying, then you know that their words are not of God. I speak from personal experiences on this matter. Let us help others build confidence, instead of picking on the supposedly weak; for we are all weak in our own ways.

Let me end on this note. I give God credit and thank Him for letting me live another day, for giving me the air to breath. I also thank Him for giving me three beautiful children. I do believe we have a soul or spirit that will one day live beyond this Earth, and I hope that in the end this spirit will reside in a place called Heaven. Perhaps one day I will feel the connection with God that others do. If that day comes to pass, I may have to retract everything I have written on the subject of God and Church. And believe me, if that day comes, I will be more than happy to do so!

THERE IS STRENGTH IN THE RIGHT CHOICES

Making good choices is the single most important element of the critical thinking process. Good choices will aid you in living the life you want to lead, and determine whether the sum character of that life is positive or negative. The wisdom of others who have gone through life before us tells us how crucial making the right choices is to living the good life. Wherever you happen to be in life, there is somebody out there who has already walked the same road. The situations of your life are not original. If you want to understand how life operates, ask someone older than you. Chances are they have been where you are, or know how to avoid the pitfalls you are at risk of falling into. The older they are, the wiser they should be.

A lot of people make choices based on logic alone. I don't rely on logic only. Logic, for example, knows that if you put your hand in a fire, it will get burned. A lot of my decision-making is based on intuition. Some people call it gut or heart, but whatever it is, it is within you, a part of yourself. I call it your soul's consciousness. Whether marrying my wife at a young age or opening a business, all my most important decisions have been made by intuition rather than logic. Logic would have told me to wait until I had a job to marry my wife, so that I could better support her while she was in school, and logic would have also told me that there is far too much risk in starting your own company. Logic may be right for a lot of other people, but it wasn't always right for me. I went with my gut and it paid off great!

I completely trust myself. I know that my instincts, my inner self, will not lead me in the wrong direction. It is my compass. We all are wired with "God-Given Common Sense." We have an inner self we consult with to determine whether we should or should not do something. There is an internal debate that goes on within yourself when making a decision, and this debate is how you justify your actions.

Of course, sometimes we use this internal debate to justify destructive actions. There is a strong instinct for self-destruction at times, what Freud called the "death-wish." I believe I had a death-wish for a long time. I was constantly in fights and pushing the boundaries set by adults. I had no fear! I have never let fear hold me back from doing or saying what I want. But the trick is to be fearless in constructive ways. Decisions based on fear can hurt others in ways we don't always anticipate. My mother and stepfather were fearful of me, and justified giving up and getting rid of me by saying they couldn't control me. When I was younger I believed their motives were purely selfish. Now, being older and wiser, I consider my mother's actions in a somewhat different light. I believe she knew she could not provide the right kind of life for me, considering all the problems I had. Yes, she said horrible things about me as a kid, but looking back, I understand that she did the right thing. Growing up, though, I despised her for giving up her "blood" son. I realize my stepfather was largely responsible for the decision to get rid of me, but ultimately, if my mother had stood up to him and said, "This is my son! I will not get rid of him!", I would have had a lot more respect for her in my youth.

"As soon as you trust yourself, you will know how to live."
Goethe

The first step of being in tune with your soul is learning to become aware of awareness. I highly recommend the book *The Power of Now*, by Echkart Tolle. It is one of the most amazing and eye-opening books I have ever read. Learning to understand my inner self and becoming aware of my conscious processes has been life-changing for me. Here is a brief quote illustrating awareness of our conscious processes.

"OBSERVING YOUR MIND
Watch the thought, feel the emotion, observe the reaction
Notice how often your attention is in the past or the future
Nothing ever happened in the past; it happened in the Now.
Nothing will ever happen in the future; it will happen in the Now."

Tolle also warns against playing what he calls the "What If Game," which is obsessing over the "What if?" questions in your mind. "What if this happens? What if I can't make it?" These kinds of questions are based in the destructive emotion of fear.

I think of this quote when determining what is real, and I remind myself to live in the Now, instead of freaking out about tomorrow. Let's get through today first.

By asking "What If?" questions, your mind is projecting itself into an imaginary future, and by doing so is creating fear. There is no way to cope with the future, because it doesn't exist. It is a mental phantom.

"Ask yourself what problems you have right now, not those you will have next year, tomorrow, or five minutes from now. What is wrong with this moment? You can always cope with the Now, but you can never cope with the future because it doesn't exist."
 -Echkart Tolle

DON'T PLAY THE "WHAT IF" GAME!!!

Don't live your life for other people, and don't care what other people think. Gene Simmons from the famous rock band KISS once made a comment that made me laugh. He stated that he made too much money to care what people think. Obviously Simmons had too much money to care what people think. But what about those of us who aren't as financially fortunate? How should we think? We should be as free-thinking and free-flowing as the wind. It doesn't take money to ignore the negative words of others.

Don't let their negativity get stuck in your mind, just let it blow away. No one knows you the way you do. Don't let anyone criticize and demean your inner spirit.

You cannot please everyone but you can please yourself. If you take care of yourself first and become happy, this happiness will shine through. People will notice and wonder what makes you such a happy and special person. It will seem abnormal, since there are so many unhappy people walking the planet. We are either going forwards or backwards. We are always in motion. Every action is based on a choice, and the sum of these choices determines our life. It is your choice, simple as that.

POPPING A PILL
MAY MASK THE PROBLEM.

LET KIDS BE KIDS!

In a world full of negativity, people really take notice of happy people. Happiness is the ultimate goal in life. Everyone wants to feel good, and feel good right now! It seems that nobody wants to experience or deal with sadness, depression, and difficult circumstances. When most people to come face-to-face with the very real, very harsh reality that life can be overwhelming and challenging, they find themselves wanting to give up. They don't even try to **FIGHT** their way back to the happy and fulfilling life that would be possible if they showed a little more grit and determination. Especially pathetic to me is when big drug companies claim to sell happiness in a pill. Great masses of people swallow the message, then follow up by taking the easy way out and swallowing the pill. It's the popular thing to do these days. Just take a pill and you'll magically feel better. But what's so wrong with feeling crappy once in a while? Get off your butt and figure it out! Life isn't always easy or fun.

Depression might be our body's way of telling us that something in our life isn't the way it should be. If I was content to just pop pills because my mother and father kicked the crap out of me when I was a baby, then I wouldn't be a fighter today. Sometimes life just really sucks.

My innocent childhood years were violently taken from me. It often makes me mad as hell. But I don't want some pill to make me feel better. I allowed myself be justifiably angry about a bad situation, and by confronting my emotions in their rawest form, was then able to move forward by asking myself what I was going to do about it.

In my case, by allowing myself to fully feel and then overcome my anger, I was motivated to be the kind of father I never had, letting my kids know every day how much they mean to me. You reading this right now—GET MAD! Be pissed off, then get off your butt and fix the problem. Fight to make your life better!!! Never give up on fighting for the happy and fulfilling life you want.

Fake happiness pills cloud reality, and by doing so SEEM to make life easier. But I believe that these pills only mask the deeper sadness concealed underneath. Happiness cannot come from a little pill or a drink or drugs, it has to come from hard work within yourself. The fake happiness pills actually make the difficulties in life worse. When a person chooses to alter their brain chemistry it leaves both the brain and mind dependent on the quick-fix. It's so easy to take a pill and so hard to fight back and figure out what's so upsetting about your life. What most people don't realize is that the deepest and truest happiness comes from choosing the hard road, developing one's own spiritual tools and personal strength. With hardship comes the realization that you have what it takes to overcome over-whelming circumstances. This realization alone is capable of bringing happiness. I love the following quote. It is so true to life.

"Many of our fears are tissue-paper thin, and a single coura-geous step would carry us clear through them." - Brendan Francis

We have become a society so dependent on the "quick fix" that we never gain the strength that comes from courageously facing our problems. We are never able to grow, and become emotion-ally and intellectually stunted.

We become stagnant and dependent, either staying stuck in a psychological and spiritual rut, or actually going backwards in our life, reverting to immature and unhealthy modes of thinking. A lot of people pop a pill, become alcoholics or drug addicts, simply because they fear facing the truth about their own prob-lems.

This may not apply to all people, because there are certainly those who truly need the medicine to function. But I believe lots of people take the easy way out, and soon become trapped, their mind and body now dependent on the medicine. It is an addic-tion, and causes even greater mental imbalance than there would be without the pill. Especially when it is not taken properly, which is often the case. And users frequently become worse if they are finally able to overcome their dependency on the drug. It may be hard for them to enjoy a normal, healthy mental and emotional life. Their brain chemistry has been altered to the point where they now cannot do without the pills. This may lead to going back on them.

It is frightening how we let dependency and addiction control us and our children. I thank God that my parents, foster parents, and the psychiatrists working in the foster system chose not to put me on Ritalin, either to calm or dumb me down. My case file shows that I was a hyperactive little boy, and probably a prime candidate for the drug, but in their wisdom my foster parents didn't go that route. A little boy just needs to be a little boy, directed and guided and nurtured, not controlled by drugs simply so parents can more easily deal with him. It is the drug companies who profit from this deception, not the parents or children who will have to deal with all the many side-effects. Shame on the doctors who prescribe it, altering the minds and bodies of children, encouraging parents and kids alike to take the easy way out. When properly prescribed, Ritalin and other drugs may help, but abuse is rampant, and more than anything seems to be how parents avoid the responsibilities of parenting.

What are its short-term effects?

Ritalin (methylphenidate) is a central nervous system stimulant, similar to amphetamines in the nature and duration of its effects. It is believed that it works by activating the brain stem arousal system and cortex.

Pharmacologically, it works on the neurotransmitter dopamine, and in that respect resembles the stimulant characteristics of cocaine. Short-term effects can include nervousness and insomnia, loss of appetite, nausea and vomiting, dizziness, palpitations, headaches, changes in heart rate and blood pressure (usually elevation of both, but occasionally depression), skin rashes and itching, abdominal pain, weight loss, and digestive problems, toxic psychosis, psychotic episodes, drug dependence syndrome, and severe depression upon withdrawal.

What are its long-term effects?

High doses of stimulants produce a predictable set of symptoms that include loss of appetite (may cause serious malnutrition), tremors and muscle twitching, fevers, convulsions, and headaches (may be severe), irregular heartbeat and respirations (may be profound and life threatening), anxiety, restlessness, paranoia, hallucinations, and delusions, excessive repetition of movements and meaningless tasks, and formicaton (sensation of bugs or worms crawling under the skin).

Source: Indiana Prevention Resource Center (IPRC)

Life is not always about the easy way. If you always look for the easy route, you will never be strengthened by adversity. We are so concerned with pampering our kids and restricting our kids, that we don't let kids just be kids. People are too ready to restrict their kid's growth these days. When I was kid, my clothes were not the popular brands and I wore hand-me-downs. We played games and pretended like we were superheroes, cowboys, or a bunch of GI Joes. Sports teams are made absurdly politically correct or some parent will complain. Everybody gets a trophy.

We hear excuse after excuse. Everything is about excuses. I'm sure you've heard the following quotes: "We can't upset the child," or, "it will give them a complex," or, "it will make them feel insecure." Parents get upset, pushing and threatening the coaches into playing their kid. "Play them more, play them more!" How about this parents? Go push yourselves out the door, and spend time practicing with your kids on their sports abilities. Stop making excuses for your kids. Kids don't get better without practicing.

Someone needs to push them to excel. This is called developing discipline. I was bad at sports when I was younger, but became really good as I practiced. These days, everything is set up to make the kid feel good and show them the easy path to success. But they may not ever become successful on account that their life was made too easy.

Back in the old days before video games, TV, cars, air-conditioning, phones, microwaves, bicycles, computers, and every other modern convenience, there were generations who succeeded through having nothing. They were forced to become strong in the face of adversity. Nowadays everyone is so worried about their son getting scrapes and bruises that we have emasculated our boys. Society is teaching our boys to be soft. Dad's should spend time with their sons, getting off the pavement and riding bikes with them in the "dirt." Masculine fathers raise masculine sons. I'm not saying a father should teach male domination, or try and indoctrinate his son in a chauvinistic, egotistical, disrespectful, and limiting way. But a father needs to give his son the essential tools that will provide him with the ability to someday search for and respect his soul-mate. A man needs to choose a wife who will love and help raise their children in an honest and ethical way. I believe that what might be called the traditionally "masculine" posture is necessary to weathering all the modern social ills that can potentially bring our children down.

I for one sometimes have a problem with this society trying to emasculate or
"de-masculinize" our boys. Let boys be boys, like it was in the old days. Ask your Grandpa how it used to be, and he will give you an earful. How many men are "real" men these days, and not just submissive order-takers? Do a lot of men these days have traits more characteristic of femininity than masculinity? I do not want my son's to sponge those character traits. I want my son's to turn out as real masculine men. Of course I'm not talking about the development of an egotistical personality, or somebody who believes in chauvinistic male domination. This kind of manhood is a disrespectful and unrespectable trait that hurts both the men and women of this world.

Women are the queens, and I want to make sure that my son treats them as such. Being a man, to me, is not about being domineering and oppressive. A man means having courage to stand up and think freely, and therefore freely will himself to take actions in accordance with his conscience.

For those who attend church on a regular basis, try this. The next time you go, look around at your congregation and try to point out the next David. This was the boy who had the courage to face Goliath. Do we have the courage to face the many Goliaths of our own day? Our boys and men are facing a masculine identity crisis. Are our churches teaching boys and men how to be strong like the heroes of the Bible? Strong like Joseph, son of Jacob, who once was sold by his brothers into slavery. What a strong and patient man that endured pain. He was eventually freed and became the chief advisor to the Egyptian pharaoh. Or like Moses ending up adopted by a royal family. After killing an Egyptian slave master, he fled and became a shepherd and was later commanded by God to deliver the Hebrews from slavery. Moses was incredible and a man who had love for the oppressed people. I love the story of Samson. He is the perfect symbol of masculinity. He used his strength to battle against his enemies and demonstrated how strong he was compared to other men by killing an entire army, wrestling a lion, and using his physical strength to bring down a building.

But of course, strength isn't always about physical ability. Remember Jesus' right-hand man, Simon Peter, who protected Jesus from the captain and officers who had come to take him by pulling out his sword and cutting the high priests ear off. Jesus admonished him, "He who lives by the sword, dies by the sword." Spiritual strength is as necessary as physical strength in facing the challenges of today, even more so. But it is wise to remember that the two are interconnected. As Aristotle said, the goal is "a healthy mind in a healthy body."

Jesus, of course, serves as a great example of a spiritual hero. He was a teacher, healer and performer of miracles. But he was also a carpenter. I have yet to see a carpenter who does not look masculine. Are our churches teaching us how to be masculine? Or are they teaching us to not have a backbone and do what they say without question? For some reason, while at church I've noticed how many tired, weak and submissive people there are.

They don't really appear to be happy or enjoying themselves. They seem to not be letting their wonderful and uplifting personalities shine through. You would think that they'd be happy while rejoicing in the worship of God. They sometimes remind me of drones, zombies or robots that are programmed to follow and not to think for themselves. Religion should be one more institution encouraging manliness and courageous spirituality. Not simply as "defenders of the faith," but as true heroes in our everyday lives.

Ask yourselves, Moms and Dads, "Do I want my kids to turn out like me?" So many parents are about "quality time" with their kids, which often turns out to be no more than fifteen "quality" minutes a day. That's nothing! I believe there should be as much emphasis on "quantity time" with children. I used to be the workaholic father who would see his kids no more than a few minutes a day, and sometimes not at all if I went to work before they got up and came home after they were asleep. I would justify this neglect by saying, "That's just the way it is; I am working hard to provide for them." I was this kind of man until my wife lovingly convinced me that the kids needed a father in their lives, and that she would be more than happy moving from our big home into a much smaller one. I realized that with better time management I could make it home much earlier. At first when I started getting home earlier, it was a little uncomfortable. I felt like I needed to be working, and wasn't really able to give the attention to my kids. Sometimes I felt like the kids liked Mommy better than me. I realized that I needed to build a relationship with my children, and it wasn't going to come overnight. I was committed to this family, and needed to show them that Daddy loved them and would spend lots of time making life more enjoyable for all of us. Over the past few years, I have developed into a much better father, and my relationship with my children is one the things about my life that makes me happiest. Remember, sometimes it's quantity over quality with your children. Just ask them. They'll tell you that they would love to see you more than they do.

Now the question is, Are you a boring Dad? Moms, are you loving enough to your children? Do you want your kids to settle for a boring, unhappy life? Or do you want to help develop their passions, unbridle them, and inspire them to push through the boundaries and barriers that would keep them from an adventurous life?

Life is an adventure. You only get one chance. Don't take away your children's opportunity to do something great with their life. They are trusting you to mold and develop them. If you don't, your child will harbor ill feelings towards you and resent the fact that you may have stunted their growth. They will hold you accountable. I have heard unhappy kids say, "My dad doesn't spend any time with me," or, "My Mom works too much." Dads need to loosen up and be boys themselves.

Regarding me, my wife always says that "boys will always be boys." Even if you have girls, play with them in the dirt. Expose your sons and daughters to the natural world. Let them hold a snake, help them catch a lizard or a spider. Put it in a clear jar and watch it spin its web. Let them ride a horse so that they can feel the spirit of that beautiful animal. Take them fishing. Have them shoot a bow and arrow, or take them to a gun range to shoot a real gun. Go camping or boating with them. Take them rafting down a river. Go to the ocean, cook a meal on a campfire. Go on a real hike in some state park, not just a walk on the pavement to your local park. The point is, get these kids away from television, video games, and the computer. Get into playing in the great soil of this Earth. There is a huge, beautiful landscape that will teach your kids to appreciate creation. Love your children. Laugh with them, be silly with them. You are so lucky to have them. There are so many couples who can't have children. Happiness is contagious, sadness is hellacious.

Get your sons and daughters outside. Have them help you pull weeds from your yard, or better yet, have them help your neighbor. Back in the old days, kids were more likely to help others. These days' parents do almost everything for their kids. But kids need to learn how to work and help out. My last foster family made me work. We lived on a farm, so I had to pull my own weight. I was given the responsibility of feeding the many animals, milking the goats, collecting the chicken eggs, shoveling animal poop, weeding, digging holes, and planting vegetables. I also had inside chores like dishes, cleaning bathrooms, vacuuming and mopping. I see kids in our society doing homework and playing sports on the weekend, but where is the work?

Do you allow your child to slip out of doing the real work necessary to maintaining your house? I'm talking about more than emptying the dishwasher or picking up their own clothes.

Kids need the discipline that hard work brings. I believe parents are doing a major disservice by not allowing their children to pull their own weight. Give them responsibilities so they know what it's like to have pressures on them. If you baby them, they will act like babies as adults, whether at their jobs or in their marriages. Then they adopt the "poor me" syndrome. We need to train our children to be honest, self-motivated, self-sufficient, and to have a great work ethic. It is imperative that they have the strength to make it in this cruel and crazy world.

I say the kids in our culture need to "man up" and stop being protected. I know, I am guilty of protecting my kids. I justified this by saying, "I just want my child to have it better than I had it," and, "I want my kids to have more than I did." But I came to the realization that I was starting to raise spoiled children who had the mentality of "give me, give me, and give me more!" I did give because I could. That was a mistake and my wife and I quickly remedied the situation. We realized our kids needed to work and learn the value of a hard-earned dollar. Even though my kids are all under the age of seven, they now understand the power of working hard and contributing to the family, while also earning a few extra dollars to buy what they want from the store. They also understand that if they spend their money on a candy bar, they may not have enough money to buy a Hot Wheel. They have become very choosy about what they purchase. They now value the dollar. They also know that Mom and Dad are not going to just buy them whatever they want.

Occasionally I buy my children a special little surprise, but they understand that they need to work in order to make their own purchases. They earn money by picking up snails from my garden for five cents a piece, or pulling up weeds. I pay them a dollar for every five-gallon bucket they fill. Now they sometimes join me when I'm working out in the yard. They know they aren't getting paid, but that they're contributing to the family, and that families work together without any pay or reward other than making the house look nice. These days parents often choose to do the work their kids should be doing, just so they don't have to argue with their children. Sometimes it feels like a bigger chore to get the child motivated than to just do the chore oneself. What do you think the end result will be if this continues?

Men are made, not born. Life is not always about the easy way. If you always look for the easy route, you will pass this same philosophy on to your children. Don't wish for things to be easier, force yourself to be better! What we think is freeing us is really enslaving us!

CHILD ABUSE
TRAPPED IN SAD MEMORIES

Child abuse is incomprehensibly hurtful and damaging to a child. I have been on the receiving end of child abuse and it has haunted me throughout my life. I'm not talking about a spanking once in a while. I am talking about inflicting severe pain on a child with the intent to cause physical trauma. I am talking about an out of control adult inflicting horrific pain on their own flesh and blood, a helpless little kid. Most mothers and fathers would do anything for their children, even die for them, but some soulless mothers and fathers are more than willing to hurt their kids mentally and physically.

I still remember very vividly one of the most horrific abuse incidents which ever happened to me. It is so embedded in my soul that it feels as if it just happened yesterday. I will take you there with me now.

It was a sunny day in California. The year was 1975. I was a kindergartner. I was a curious and tough five year-old boy. My mother, stepfather, half-brother, half-sister and I lived in a two story townhouse. There was nice green grass in the front of the house. When you walked inside, you saw the dining room and kitchen on the right and the family room on the left. In front of you was a staircase with a black iron banister leading to the bathroom and the bedrooms. The bathroom was located at the top of the stairs. The house was furnished and I remember the wood being very dark with big lamps made out of clear orange textured glass.

On the table and kitchen counter there would always be empty yellow Coors beer cans. I remember seeing lots of yellow Coors beer cans in those days.

I would often be outside playing in the tunnels under the main road overpass near our house. As a kid I called them tunnels but as an adult looking back, they were big storm drain pipes that went under the street.
I am amazed that my Mom would let me wander and play over there at such a young age. I would love to hang out there and throw rocks at the metal siding of the pipes. When the rocks would hit, it would make a cool high-pitched noise that would echo through the tunnels. It would be exciting to sit under the overpass and hear the cars go honking by overhead.
Sometimes I would find dead rats in there and lots of interest-ing junk. At times, adults would walk through, using the tun-nels as a shortcut. Older kids would sometimes hang out in them. If I was alone, the tunnels would scare me a little, but I was tough and showed no fear.

One day, it was starting to get dark and I decided to head home. When I entered the townhouse, I could hear an argu-ment going on between my mother and stepfather. I also remember a few yellow Coors beer cans. My mother asked me to do something. I defied her and said, "Screw you!" but really using the F-word. This wasn't the first time I had said these words to my mother. In fact the F-word was one of my favorite words at that age. But this time when I said it, my mother snapped, apparently having had enough of my disrespectful language. With anger in her eyes, she grabbed my arm and tried to pull me up the stairs. I resisted and fought back. I was yelling and she was yelling. It was very chaotic.

I was hitting her and she was hitting me, but eventually she overpowered me. She pulled me up the stairs to the bathroom and physically forced me to the sink. While holding me there, she turned on the hot water full blast, running it until the steam was rising profusely. She kept yelling at me, screaming that I was never to use the F-word again, telling me how bad a kid I was. She emphasized how terrible a kid I was over and over again. I remember her yelling at me uncontrollably. I think she must have totally snapped. What she did next was incomprehensible. She restrained my body and forced my tiny left hand under the scalding hot water.

I was screaming, out of control and trying to pull my hand out of the water. It hurt so much as she held it there. I screamed "Mommy stop, Mommy stop!" I was crying so loud, it hurt so much. I could not believe my own mother was doing this to me. It was like my life was flashing before my eyes and my whole body was shutting down. It was like she never heard me. I then yelled "Mommy, you're hurting me, it hurts mommy, let me go, I love you." I tried to get away but she looked at me with intense anger and said I was a bad kid. I thought I could get away, that I was stronger than her.

But I couldn't. I was only five years old. I was helpless and completely at her mercy. The skin on the back of my left hand was burned off. I have had this scar ever since, on my body, in my heart, and in my mind.

All the other physical abuse I could deal with, but this particular incident altered me physically and mentally forever. This was the final ticker for the time bomb that was about to go off. I was no longer an innocent little boy. I was now overcome with a sense of shame and anger that would last for years. I realized I was no longer good enough and that I was not really loved. I felt worthless and unwanted.

I now hated my mother. I hated her for not sticking up for me, and for not loving me. I hated her for hurting me. I was her son. Hate is such a powerful word and I don't use it lightly, but if there are two people that I hated, it was my mother and stepfather. I can't say that I hated my father because I don't remember him, but my mother was supposed to protect and love me. I recently discovered from the case files on me that my biological father brutally abused me during my first year as a baby. Can you believe that? The wording is "Brutally abused." This was my biological father. How evil is that?

I stop here and ask God, "Why did you place me with this family?" Why God, are innocent children born into such terrible situations?" Born to drug-addicted parents, sexually abusive parents, physically abusive parents, and alcoholic parents. These people are so selfish! They can't think beyond themselves or realize how they are hurting and stunting the mental growth of their child. I can't stand the fact that they put themselves and their addictions before their children. If the cycle is not broken, each generation only gets worse.

There are too many distractions nowadays, pulling parents away from their children. These children don't have the good role models who could help them break the cycle. Most of them will become a product of their environment. It is unfortunate, but a good many parents don't deserve to be parents. They don't deserve to be the caretakers of Heaven's Angels. Each child is born pure and precious. They only want to be loved and they want to please their parents. They don't know negative feelings or words until their parents start showing them what a negative word or feeling means, and the child eventually mirrors the parent's example. Everything you do or don't do with your kid molds them. What was once a pure and precious little angel can turn into an uncontrollable and aggressive little monster. I know this because my mother thought I was a devil. Sons and daughters want and deserve love from their mother and father no matter what. It doesn't matter how mean their parents are. They just want attention and love. Even as children grow into adults, they still yearn for the love and approval of their parents. I always wanted and desired my mother's love. Even as an adult, I just wanted to be validated by her.

Let's face it, I was a mistake. I was never supposed to be born. I'm sure my mother was frustrated when she accidentally became pregnant by a man who had so many emotional problems, a history of violence, who was a thief and convicted felon. Now I understand people can change for the better after making bad choices, but only IF THEY WANT TO. It appears that my biological father was never going to learn and was doomed to be a loser. My mother had to be frustrated for putting herself in that situation, and was unable to live with the consequences: me. I felt that I was a mistake, and that she was going to make me pay for it every time I behaved badly. I couldn't believe my own mother would hurt me as badly as she did, or be so vindictive.

I remember the pain. I feel the pain. I smell the pain and I see the pain. Never will I forget the memory of what was done to that innocent little five year-old boy. It is difficult to really describe the feeling of the hot scalding water burning off the majority of the skin on the top of my left hand. You could literally pull off parts of my flesh. It was awful!

I remember how angry my mother was. I wondered why I received this new kind of punishment. I kept asking, why has my mom hurt me so bad? I remember looking up at my mom and seeing her reflection in the mirror, the intense look she had, she was so focused on hurting me and taking out all of her frustration. No wonder I was diagnosed as emotionally disturbed or a "bad kid." I was a product of my environment.

This particular abusive event has followed me throughout my life. It has literally haunted me every time I take a shower. Before I get into the shower, I'll test the water with my hand to make sure it isn't too hot. Every time I touch the water, it automatically takes me back to the moment when my mother held my hand under the scalding water. It was uncontrollable. I could not block it out of my mind. I just lived it over and over every day of my life. It was like a broken record, constantly repeating over and over again. I had to make sure the water wasn't hot. I would look at my left hand and remember the skin burnt off and the pink color that showed beneath.

I would also recall this horrific event every time I washed dishes, got into a hot tub, or washed my hands. If the water even had the possibility of being hot, I would recall the awful memory of being burned. I have thought about what my mother did to me every single day of my life, ever since the day it occurred.

I believe this was the greatest obstacle to me attaining complete happiness with myself at an early age. This unhappiness followed me everywhere. Anger would flow through my heart, then sadness.   Every day I had to relive that experience, and it would put me in a negative frame of mind. If I could not get over it quickly enough, this negativity would color my entire day, affecting others around me.

As a child and teenager I tried many different forms of therapy. But there is one particular kind of therapy which worked amazingly well in ridding me of the fear of hot water. I highly recommend it to others. It is called EMDR (Eye Movement and Desensitization and Reprocessing)

HOW DOES EMDR WORK?

"No one knows how any form of psychotherapy works neuro-biologically, or in the brain. However, we do know that when a person is very upset, their brain cannot process information as it does ordinarily. One moment becomes 'frozen in time,' and remembering a trauma may feel as bad as going through it the first time because the images, sounds, smells, and feelings haven't changed. Such memories have a lasting negative effect that interferes with the way a person sees the world and the way they relate to other people."

WHAT IS THE ACTUAL EMDR SESSION LIKE?

During EMDR, the therapist works with the client to identify a specific problem as the focus of the treatment session. The client calls to mind the disturbing issue or event, what was seen, felt, heard, thought, etc., and what thoughts and beliefs are currently held about the event. The therapist facilitates the directional movement of the eyes or other dual attention simu-lation of the brain, while the client just notices whatever comes to mind without making any effort to control direction or con-tent. Sets of eye movements are continued until the memory becomes less disturbing and is associated with positive thoughts and beliefs about one's self.
During EMDR, the client may experience intense emotions, but by the end of the session, most people report a great reduc-tion in the level of disturbance.

WHAT KIND OF PROBLEMS CAN EMDR TREAT?

Scientific research has established EMDR as effective for post traumatic stress. However, clinicians have also reported success using EMDR in treatment of the following conditions:
personality disorders
panic attacks
complicated grief
disassociative disorders
disturbing memories
phobias
pain disorders
eating disorders
performance anxiety
stress reduction
addictions
sexual and/or physical abuse
body dysmorphic disorders

The above information on EMDR was from a pamphlet from the EMDR Internal Association.
Website: www.emdria.org

Another unfortunate event happened to me when I was about five years old. I sometimes had a problem wetting my bed, or if I was mad at my parents I would pee on their things. That was my way of telling them I didn't want to be treated the way they were treating me. If I wet my bed the night before, my stepfather would become very angry with me. So he'd pull me over to the toilet and force my head into the bowl. He would stand over me and push my head down, forcing me to stay there. Now I didn't ever come close to drowning, but it wasn't a nice thing to do to another human being. He was treating me like a misbehaving dog or animal. He probably considered me an animal. He did not like me. I was the middle child, putting major pressure and stress on his marriage to my mother. He had his own son, the youngest, and I was now the bad seed. I'm sure he was nice to me in the beginning, at least until he won my Mom over.

Well this one time when he was sticking my head into the toilet, my mother heard the commotion. He was yelling at me about peeing my bed, telling me how angry he was. My Mom told him to stop holding my head down. There was a huge argument, and in the heat of it all, as he was forcing my head into the toilet, she grabbed my left hand and yanked my arm back. She yanked it so hard that she caused shoulder damage. I cannot tell you if it was dislocated, or if something was ripped or broken, but it was so painful that she made me a sling to hold my arm up. Years later, I still have pain in my shoulder, and it always rests higher than the other one. Every morning I have to try and force my bad shoulder down and stretch it out so that it's comfortable throughout the day.

At least after that day, my stepfather stopped putting my head in the toilet. Abuse is hard to live with, but fortunately I am a fighter. I am a conqueror who has set his mind free. Life isn't fair. The only thing I can control is my attitude and outlook on it. My philosophy and motto are simple: I WILL NEVER GIVE UP!

I wrote this poem when I was a senior in high school, soon after my brother and sister were killed. I was flooded with doubts about me being loved, and questioned my own ability to make the choices which would secure me a better life. This is a collection of the recurring thoughts that kept going through my mind. I found it very helpful to turn my emotions into art, to have an expressive outlet for them, so that I could then analyze them and see if they were making any sense, and whether or not they exposed certain negative or destructive tendencies. And if so, whether my artistic expression also revealed a way to overcome them.

"Waiting nine months, waiting for their bundle of joy, then from the time after birth, the mother and father are in fear of what they created.

A second child to an alcoholic family,
his name is Derek Clark,
completely innocent, not knowing of his future calamity.

Well the boy started to grow,
And soon learned to talk,
The parents weren't excited about his achievements,
They would rather go for a walk.
Left him in the house with his older sister,
Seeing the Coor's beer cans
Never see his parents hit her.

Why would they hit him,
Why such abuse,

He was only one to four years old,
Not believing he had much use.
He once told his mom the F word,
She took him upstairs
To the bathroom and turned on the hot water
And held his hand under there.
With the hot water burning the skin off his left hand,
He was screaming for Mom,
But she didn't understand.

Leaving scars for life,
That will add to his nightmare,
Someday will affect his future,
If he doesn't learn to care.

They took all their anger,
Used him like a whipping boy,
Hit things against his head,
Threw him down the stairs like a toy.

When the boy was five,
The parents said he was out of control,
Off to Snedigar Cottage,
Where his life would begin to take its toll.
Staying there, he felt all alone
Then he got transferred to a foster home.

No need to feel all alone,
All he ever wanted

Was to be back home.

Alcohol was the source
Of this young boys detrimental childhood,
Never will he do the same to his kids,
Pain was something he understood.

So as a teenager,
The nightmare is still there,
Sweating the fear in his sleep,
Living the little boy's nightmare.

With scars to look at
And recalls of the past
This boy is making his own life
One about which he will be
Pleased at last."

MY MUSIC IS MY THERAPY

Music is simply amazing. Next to my family, my music is the most important thing in my life. I am not talking about going to concerts or turning on the radio. I mean creating music from the wellspring of the soul. My testimony of life, my faith and my beliefs are expressed through the musical melodies circulating around my soul. My sadness, anger and happiness are turned into a song, where they become almost as precious to me as the children I have created. I can't tell you which song is my favorite. It's like telling you which of my kids is my favorite. It is impossible to say, but I can tell you that creation is in tune with the music of your heart. Music can change the mood you're in from sadness and anger to an energetic happiness. Finding just the right sound can bring tears to your eyes. When composed with passion, music is nothing less than miraculous. It can literally heal the emotionally wounded.

I will always be indebted to my foster father for passing the miracle of music on to me. I started learning music when I was about eight years old. My foster father played piano and would teach me the basics of music theory and accompany me on duets. He also laid the foundation for me never giving up. He never let me quit when it became hard to learn. Sometimes I couldn't stand playing the clarinet. But he would make me memorize pages of music for performances.

I didn't like it much then, but I eventually got very good at memorizing pieces and playing them well, which helped me blossom into a competent musician, giving me confidence and greatly increasing my self-esteem.

He was committed to teaching me the love of music, and would work with me twice a day in an effort to help me improve. He put me in private lessons for years and made sure that I was enrolled in the school band.

I played the clarinet for years. I got very good at that clarinet and won some major competitions at the university level when I was only twelve years old. I wasn't born with the ability to play music. It was a lot of hard, agonizing work. That licorice stick (clarinet) became my buddy and we became one. I soon became recognized as an accomplished clarinet player. The fact that people liked what I was doing and the person I was becoming helped bolster my sense of self-worth. I am indebted to my foster father for never giving up on me, and passing his talent down. Now I can pass the love of music on to my own children.

Music has dramatically changed my life. It has given me the ability to express feelings which otherwise would have remained locked in my soul. Music was the key to the cell that I was trapped in. Music is literally like another language. Playing music is fun, but creating music can change your life. The feeling that overcomes you when you're inspired to create and let your soul breathe free can leave you stunned. It is true inspiration. When you attain the musical ability that allows you to express your deepest emotions, you can sit with a guitar in your hand and sing about what you are feeling at any given moment. It is beautiful how the words just flow out.

When I was eight years old, I decided right then and there that someday I was going to be a rock star, and everyone would like me and love my music. Well, I never became a rock star in the world's eyes, but I am a rock star to my own children. They absolutely love that I play music to them. I also learned that not everyone is going to like my music and that you can't go through life always looking for other people's approval and acceptance. I admit that's a tough thing to accept sometimes, because everyone wants to be liked and I'm no different in this regard. Being a foster kid makes you feel rejected, and you consider yourself unworthy. Music was the vehicle which allowed me to open up and dream. Dreams can give you hope, and hope was the only thing I needed.

Music has taught me appreciation for the little things. My music gives form to the feelings I have inside. When I am inspired to write, it comes from some deep place in the heart. I have had many opportunities to sing my songs in public performances and see how the music effects others. It is humbling to know that one of my songs can comfort another person, and give them strength to endure a hard time. That is one of the main reasons I like country music. If you ever want to get real and simple, turn on a country radio station and listen to the words of these songs. They write graciously about simple, everyday situations that effect people.

It may be a song about a child stricken with cancer, a son's view of a step dad, death of a loved one, first love, family bonds, loving America and starting your life all over again. People connect with music. I am not ashamed to have cried numerous times while listening to a song that touched me deeply. In fact, there was a time when on Saturday mornings I would turn on the TV and watch country music videos, and would consistently have a Saturday morning cry. It used to be a joke between my wife and I, when I'd say "Honey, I just had my Saturday morning cry."

Music has helped me to get in tune with other people and come to know their spirits, needs and intentions. It has helped me stay grounded and real. It has allowed me to maintain a connection with my soul and spirit, instead of shunning or hating myself. I like myself and love myself, not in some self-absorbed manner that makes me egotistical or narcissistic, but in a way that allows me to be proud of how far I have come. I like that for most of my life I have gone forwards instead of backwards, and that I try everyday to improve myself in some way.

I have written personally revealing songs since I was seventeen years old. The following song lyrics have been put to music and professionally recorded. I have decided to share them with you so that you may see how I expressed myself during some difficult times.

I wrote "I Wanna Be A Kid" when I was thirty years old. My wife and I had been married for seven years at that point, and decided we wanted to have a child. This was a huge deal and a big step for me. Before we were married we discussed the possibility of not having children.

I was a product of a messed up relationship and therefore had a messed up childhood. I was reluctant to bring any more children into this evil and cruel world. When we decided to have a child, she was pregnant within a month. "Holy cow, that was very quick," I said. I was shocked and grew very scared wondering what kind of father I was going to be. I felt unworthy to take care of a baby angel. I was facing a flood of emotions and bad memories. I could feel the little foster kid inside me beginning to cry. I felt vulnerable. I decided to write a song to my mom, to show her that I can be a winner, and that nobody was going to stop me from soaring in my life. This song has been an inspiration to many. This is my anthem. Its message is that if I can make it in life, then anybody can make it. I have been questioned about the meaning of the chorus, which says "Bunk to Bombay." It means a bunk bed to somewhere far away. I was tired of bunk beds at the foster homes. I just wanted to escape. If you go to my website www.iwillnevergiveup.com you can hear this song and watch the music video.

This song has touched so many people. The following email was written by a military psychologist serving in Iraq, describing how they felt about the song:

"Everyone in the platoon, including myself, has never known a mother. There is only one of us who knew their Dad. Everyone in the platoon grew up in foster care and orphanages. Nobody is complaining. Let's just say we all came up through the school of hard knocks. When the platoon heard Derek Clarke's song "I Wanna Be a Kid," they all wept tears that were long in coming;

very needed and very healing. This song has become our platoon anthem and we listen to it several times a day. Recently myself and another US Marine, Kong, were WIA (Wounded in Action). During the course of getting medical evacuation from a fire-fight, we both had a surreal experience. As Kong and I floated in and out of consciousness, we both had a vision of a huge angel coming to us, telling us to hang on, and throughout the time this angel was present, we heard Derek singing the words to his song, "I Wanna Be a Kid." The music was so loud it was like we had a $400 Bose head-set clamped on our heads. The pure, pristine sound of Derek singing that song played over and over as we were taken care of by the medics and taken to the combat hospital. The angel kept saying, 'Listen to the song, there is more to come....' The platoon and I feel his words "I wanna fly" symbolize the freedom found in conquering the past with the help of God and his angels, and flying free to a better future." – Dr. Ariane T. Alexander "Doc"

I WANNA BE A KID

BY DEREK W.CLARK

You want to see me cry, you want to see me die,
You want to look into my eyes
And see the devil's eyes,
You want to see me smile with my battle scars

But if you look into my eyes,
You'll see an Angel's heart,
It was 1975, I was 5,
Momma I was looking at you all surprised
But you were looking at me with fear,
And all along Momma, you didn't want me here.

(Chorus)
I wanna fly, bunk to Bombay,
Here I am in this world today,
I wanna fly, bunk to Bombay
Here I am, I need a home today.
No more Foster Homes and no more Orphanage,
I just wanna be a kid.

So here I am in the struggle of the human race,
But no one wants me, my face, I feel so disgraced,
I'm just an orphan in line, like a lamb to a slaughter,
I could be a good son, but no one bothers,
Well the good Lord works in mysterious ways,
He opened Heavens gates for only one day,
And the Angels of courage and Love were sent,
There was this one loving Family, that took me in.

(Chorus)
I wanna fly, bunk to Bombay,
Here I am in this world today,
I wanna fly, bunk to Bombay
Here I am, I need a home today.
No more Foster Homes and no more Orphanage,
I just wanna be a kid.

I've got a sad past, everyday a ghost haunts me,
They can't harm me, I've got a family,
I've got a son, a wife, I've got a true life,
It's been given back to me, I'll do it right,
They'll never live the Hell that I have been through,
I can guarantee that, I swear to you,
This is real, this is my life,
If I can fly, you can fly.

(chorus)
I wanna fly, bunk to Bombay,
Here I am in this world today,
I wanna fly, bunk to Bombay
Here I am, I need a home today.
No more Foster Homes and no more Orphanage,
I just wanna be a kid.
Don't leave me alone Mom.
I just wanna be a kid.
Don't leave me alone Mom

"Head Up High" was a pinnacle song for me. It allowed me to express myself from the perspective of an adult, instead of from a little boy's point of view. As adults we tend to attach meaning to our suffering and bring the pain of the past into our current life. I felt that I was in the crossfire of suffering again, because having this little child reminded me of myself when I was a child. This was another song I wrote after having my first baby. It is about getting past my own demons so that I could concentrate on raising a pure boy with no lingering issues that would negatively affect his upbringing.

HEAD UP HIGH
BY
DEREK W. CLARK

I don't feel sorry for my life,
but it poisons my mind.
I'm lying naked on the bathroom floor,
Oh Lord, I think I need you so more.
Help me, I'm depressed.
Help me, I'm a mess.
I need some strength, to spread my wings.
I see your footprints in my dreams.
Jesus talks to me,
Keep your head up high.

(Chorus)
Head up high
because this boy is free
Head up high
because this boy is free
Head up high

Maybe you can lift me higher
Head up high
because this boy is free

No more tears.
No more pain.
Let misery go away.
My son is going to see me cry someday.
If I cry son, forgive me,
the Lords working on setting me free.

(Chorus)
Head up high
because this boy is free
Head up high
because this boy is free
Head up high
Maybe you can lift me higher
Head up high
because this boy is free

Head up,
Maybe you could learn how to fly
Head up
Maybe you could learn how to fly
Head up,
Son may you could fly
Head up,
Son maybe you could fly

"Reach For Me" is a song about reaching out to my mother during a hellish time. This song has to do with literally living in hell as a state of mind. Sometimes when you are there, you don't know how to get out of your self-imprisonment, so you reach out and hope that somebody grabs you.

REACH FOR ME
BY
DEREK W. CLARK

Lightning strikes in my heart one more time.
I want you to breathe my soul.
Isn't it enough that I disappear from your life.
Reach for me,
My self destruction is for you.

Reach for me

I'm lucky to be alive.
I want you to sacrifice me.
I feel nothing from you now,
but your demons that are dieing in me.
You once said I couldn't be a man,
but I struggle everyday being superman.
Get out of my head.

Reach for me
9 times out of 10,
I could fall again.
I've seen the light
I'd had the faith,
I've turned to darkness
and seen the face.
No one wants to help,
when someone needs a hand.
But won't you help,
Reach for me.

This song was written while contemplating whether or not my mother really loved me. And if she didn't love me, why didn't she just put me out of my misery? This song was me crying out for her to acknowledge me, feel my pain, and tell me that she loved me.

I'M FOR REAL MOM!
BY
DEREK W. CLARK

Sometimes I'm lonely
No one understands me

I loved you but you didn't make it so easy
When you ran away scared like a little girl.
So I bulletproofed my soul with walls of emotional steel
And my eyes see deeper than you will ever feel
I long for you to cry on my heavy shoulder.

(Chorus)

I'm for real,
Hold me
Or break me down
And kill me please
I'm for real,
Feel me in your soul
I'm for real,
Love me
Look in my eyes and tell me you really love me, for real
I'm for real
I want to crawl in my little shell and
I wonder if you'd follow me back from the depths of hell,
Would you crawl back on your knees to help me live.
I don't know who I am,
I need your help
I need you to find me
Because I just lost myself,
I'm alone, I'm alone without you.

(Chorus)

I'm for real,
Hold me
Or break me down
And kill me please
I'm for real,
Feel me in your soul
I'm for real,
Love me
Look in my eyes and tell me you really love me, for real
I'm for real
I'm for real
Love me
Look in my eyes and tell me you really love me, for real
I'm for real, I'm for real.

"Everything is Nothing" was written at the point in my life when I had achieved financial success. I had become consumed with making money, and recognized that the longer hours I worked, the more money I would make. I thought I was happy. But I realized one day that, though I had all the toys and money in the bank, the relationship with my wife and children was suffering. I was not happy. I did not have the balance of family in my life. I justified long hours at work by telling myself I was providing for my family, but the truth is that my wife and children didn't care how big our house was, what car I drove, or how much more money I could put in the bank. They just wanted their husband and Daddy home.

I wanted to love, but I had lost myself. I had everything, but I was alone. This song expresses the guilt I felt as I was trying to get myself back together and remind myself what is really important in life.

It was a hard cycle to break. I felt like I had a disease, and couldn't shake off being addicted to work. It was hard for me to love, and to think of anyone besides myself. I had lost touch with my soul, spirituality, and family. I was more interested in my image, what people thought about me, and how successful I was than I was with what was REAL. What was "REAL," was that I had a beautiful family at home. I had everything a man could want; a beautiful and supportive wife who continually took care of me, a wonderful child, and all the extra material possessions. I realized I was building an empire of DIRT and nothing more. Everything comes from dirt, and everything returns to dirt. I couldn't take any of the material possessions with me when I died. There is no luggage rack attached to my coffin. How much of your value is based on material and external wealth, rather than internal wealth? I thought, "What would my family remember about me if I was to die?

Was I a great husband and a loving father who spent time with his family? Was I putting enough time into what I valued most?" I can honestly say that I now have my priorities straight. Through this storm of adversity, I grew as a human being. I thank my wife and children for their constant support and for never giving up on me.

EVERYTHING IS NOTHING
BY
DEREK W. CLARK

I'd bleed for you, I'd die for you
I'd live the rest of my life, to grow old with you
But the angels don't cry for me
Because I am one of those diseased
And there's no way out from destroying my self
These prison walls are falling on me

(Chorus)
Everything is nothing
I'm feeling all alone
Everything is darkness

Why can't I feel love
You crucified me for what I was
I'd die a real slow death
So you could hear what I'd say in my last breath
And the angels they want to see

All the love that I got in me
I want to give it to you but I don't know how
I want to find what you really want in me

(Chorus)
Everything is nothing
I'm feeling all alone
Everything is fragile
My heart has almost stopped
Everything is darkness
The light is almost gone
Everything is nothing
It's nothing to me

Well life has a way of digging up the past
And these bones shatter like glass
I think I'm crazy or scared of me
Somebody help, I have a disease.

(Chorus)
Everything is nothing
I'm feeling all alone
Everything is fragile
My heart has almost stopped
Everything is darkness
The light is almost gone
Everything is nothing
It's nothing to me

"Goodbye to Goodbyes" was very recently written, just before I started this book. I had just looked at my case file with the county regarding my past as a five year-old kid. I was very sad for two days after seeing how this kid had come into this world.

I felt that I finally needed to say goodbye to the past and move on. I didn't want to pass this "history disease" on to my kids. I realized that a part of me enjoyed the pain of my past, and that it might swallow me up and turn me into a person I never wanted to be. I realized that carrying all this weight was holding me down. I felt like a huge, successful, strong train that was carrying this fifty ton magnet which only allowed me to go forward a little at a time. If I could release this giant magnet, I could go so much faster as a train on the way to its destinations in life. Now I want to be a speeding train. If I allowed my pain to rule my mind, my kids would pick up on it and possibly make it theirs. So I took that pain and anguish and finally released it. I had a sad day of acknowledging my past and who I was, and it took a little while to realize that I'm not that person anymore. That was a five year-old kid and I could no longer let that kid have a voice in my head or play a part in my emotions. I decided to look forward and move on.

GOODBYE TO GOODBYES
BY
DEREK W.CLARK

(verse 1)
I've been living here on empty for 36 years,
Seen the life of a lonely man addicted to my fears.
And the hardest part of living is goodbye,
Well I learned this lesson hard when I was 5.

(chorus)
So goodbye to goodbyes,
The hardest part of living is saying goodbye,
I've seen the lonely eyes in my window,
Held the tears of a forgotten son,
I cried for days when my brother died and
Never said goodbye to mama
When she gave me up, goodbye.

(verse 2)
I've been looking back at the picture
Of how I painted my tainted life.
Have I held back love to my wife and children
For the fear of loss in goodbye.
Have I let my fear control me, oh yeah,
Now I've got one life to live,
No more wasting it, no more regrets.

(chorus)
So goodbye to goodbyes,
The hardest part of living is saying goodbye,
I've seen the lonely eyes in my window,
Held the tears of a forgotten son,
I cried for days when my brother died and
Never said goodbye to mama
When she gave me up, goodbye.

(verse 3)
On a lonely road to nowhere
Where your pity leads the way,

Is a man that lost his soul to live,
Where he drinks his life away,
And the memories hard to swallow it all down
When you're a million miles away
Where no one is found.

(chorus)
So goodbye to goodbyes,
The hardest part of living is saying goodbye,
I've seen the lonely eyes in my window,
Held the tears of a forgotten son,
I cried for days when my brother died and
Never said goodbye to mama
When she gave me up, goodbye.

"Goodnight Soldier" was written in the middle of the night, after watching a documentary about the last letter a family received from their son after he was killed in Iraq. I was heartbroken watching it. I was so very touched. My wife and I cried and cried throughout the show. It actually put a human face on the soldier, as opposed to the desensitized descriptions you hear on the news: "Six soldiers were killed today." There is rarely a name or a face to go along with the clip. When we actually saw the face, and got to know in some small way a soldier who was killed, I was powerfully moved. I realized just how extraordinary the sacrifice is that our soldiers make in defending our country. I believe the entire country should come together and show appreciation for our military. They don't get paid much for what they do, and they put everything on the line for us, including their lives.

In America, you have the right to be an anti-war advocate, but you should always support our troops. They are fighting for the right of an anti-supporter to voice his opinion. In many nations, if an anti-supporter voices his opinion, he or she could be put in prison or put to death. Because soldiers fight for you, you are afforded the opportunity to live your life the way you want. This is a beautiful country, and offers us all so much. People die trying to make America their home. We are the greatest country in the world, with opportunity for all, and it didn't get this way by sitting back and doing nothing. Our forefathers had a dream. Some said it was an impossible dream, but they made their dream *your* reality.

The realization of dreams requires sacrifice. What are you willing to sacrifice? This song is patriotic tributes to the troops, thanking them for their sacrifice, letting them know that I care and respect them for defending our freedom. Freedom isn't a given; we must constantly fight for it so that the next generation can also enjoy it. If the nation one day just up and put an end to all military operations, eventually our freedom would be taken from us. Look around the world, it happens all the time. There are great people in our military, and they are the ones who protect us. They deserve respect. God bless the active service members and the veterans!

"The first time I heard 'Goodnight Soldier' was online. I honestly don't remember the circumstances, but it was only weeks after we lost Brandon (January 20, 2006). You told us the story about writing the song and then putting it away until you heard about Brandon. The day after the funeral, you brought out the song again and recorded it in honor of Brandon, and to honor all of our military. I was so touched. We all touch each other's lives in one way or another, Brandon touched you and you touched all of us in return. Thank you Derek."

-Julia Dewey Conover
Proud Marine Mom - Brandon 3/1 KIA Iraq 1-20-2006.
Forever in my heart.
Proud Navy Mom-Elyse Hawaii

I released this song the day after Brandon's funeral through an email to all of my friends as a tribute to this hero. I never expected that my simple patriotic song, reflecting my love and respect for our military brothers and sisters, Moms and Dads, and sons and daughters would get as big as it did. It is humbling to know that my heartfelt song has touched so many in their times of sadness.

GOODNIGHT SOLDIER

BY

DEREK W. CLARK

It's late at night I pray,
For the Lord to guide your way,
I've been watching news every day.
And I don't know you at all,
But look at you standing tall,
As America runs through your veins.

(Chorus)
Good night soldier, good night friend,
'Cause when I'm sleeping here at night,
You're out protecting.
Good night soldier, good night friend,
Please come home,
So I can see you again.

There's a lot of mom and dads who care,
Everyone's a son and daughter out there,

Man, I've cried with love for you all.
I've seen a lot of halo's in the sky,
Lord bless the one's who have died,
Can you tie a yellow ribbon around us all?

(Chorus)
Good night soldier, good night friend,
'Cause when I'm sleeping here at night,
You're out protecting.
Good night soldier, good night friend,
Please come home,
So I can see you again.

DEATH IS REAL!

I have never liked death or goodbyes. I have lost a foster brother seven years older than I, who I considered my brother, and my blood sister who was ten years older. Foster grandmas and foster grandpas who I considered both great friends and my real grandparents.

I was sixteen years old when I found out that my blood sister was shot and killed by her brother-in-law, in some jealous rage over her filing for a divorce. She was shot in the head. This was on Mother's Day. She left behind two very young children. I had not seen or heard from her since I was five years old. When I was sixteen, I decided to write her a letter and she eventually wrote me back. She wanted to come and visit me. I wrote her back, never to hear from her again. My mother wrote to tell me the sad news of her death. I remember her being so gentle and loving to me. I hadn't seen her since I was put into a foster home. Eleven years later, I was brokenhearted to learn her life had been so brief on this Earth, and that we'd never be able to rekindle our relationship. It is unfortunate that we can never again enjoy the closeness we once shared.

My good friend in high school, and fellow soccer teammate, was killed for no reason. His father took a shotgun and killed him and his little sister while they were sleeping, then turned the gun on himself. I was in shock when the news circulated through school. I remember crying from the realization that life could be taken away at any point. It was unbelievable to think that just the day prior, I was playing soccer and joking around with him, and then the next day he was gone forever. He was a great guy, and I sorely missed him.

One of the most painful deaths was the loss of my foster brother. I was seventeen years old. He had his pilot's license and decided to fly some of his friends out for a weekend of fun. While they were flying over the Sequoia and Kings Canyon National Park, something went wrong and the plane crashed. He and a couple of his friends were killed. There was only one survivor. It was awful. My foster Dad did not allow me to see his body and I am thankful because I would not want to remember my brother in this way. I would rather think of how great a brother he was. He was so accepting of me joining his family. I remember when I moved into the new foster home, he was in the garage working, and he spoke kindly to me. He taught me how to ride motorcycles and took me camping. He was definitely an important role model in my teenage life. I found out he died when I came home at one in the morning after having been out dancing with some friends. My foster Mom and Dad were crying. I asked them what was wrong and they told me my brother had been killed in a plane crash. I was in state of unbelief. I could not believe my buddy was gone and that I wouldn't see him again in this lifetime. He had just gotten married the year before and had a lovely wife. I remember camping with them and the fun times we had.

After I heard of his death, I locked myself in my room for three days. I cried and cried. He was the only brother I had ever felt close to. I remember getting really mad at God and asking him why He'd taken away my sister and brother. One of my favorite movies at that time was *The Lost Boys*. It was about a group of young, rebellious vampires, free to do whatever they wanted. There was a new guy wanting to belong to their clique. I felt like that guy, a rebel and wanting to belong.

My brother made me feel like I belonged. He made me feel like I was his "real" brother. There was a song on the soundtrack called "Cry Little Sister," and I played that song over and over for many days. There was one line in particular that always stuck with me: "Come to your brother, thou shall not die....love is with your brother." I felt connected to my brother through this song. I was lonely. I now didn't have an older brother to take me motorcycling or camping, or for just hanging out with at his house. I remember thinking, "Well, now it's my turn to step up and fill the shoes of my older brother, and become the best brother I can be to my little foster brothers and sisters." Those were big shoes to fill, and I never could replace him.

I grew up being a rebel and was completely rebellious throughout my teenage years. But after these deaths I began to recognize that death was a very real thing. People were dying all around me. It took my brother's death to wake me up. I had thought I was invincible. I can't tell you how many times I got in fights, but it was a lot. As a teenager I had a problem with authority. My foster parents and I got in physical altercations when I was younger, and I was always challenging them. I got into shoving matches with adult church leaders and numerous fights with older teenagers. Even as a little kid, I did not respect or trust authority. I started to really evolve into a good person when my brother died. It really hit home that I was no longer invincible and that I needed to get myself together.

The death of my brother was what really started me on the road to personal change. I finally took ownership of my life and started to make better choices His death taught me that life was immeasurably valuable. I remember going to a three-day therapy seminar on how to move on from your problems and let go of your past. It was helpful, and laid the foundation for understanding myself and others.

So why am I writing all about death in this chapter? Because your life is so very precious. It is irreplaceable. You are the only person that can make it valuable. You can live your life or take your life away. You have the free will to make your life the way you want it to be. You live in the greatest country in the world and have more opportunities than most other people in this world. There are no excuses. We have all heard stories of immigrants who came to this country with nothing, only to become millionaires. All it takes is a dream and hard work to make that dream a reality. But maybe your dream isn't about being a millionaire. Still, whatever you want to be, you have the opportunity to become it in our society.

I have seen how life takes away from the young and the old. Death does not discriminate. You cannot get your life back when you die. Life is not like a video game where you get to restart it and try again. Life is invaluable and cannot be bought back.

All the money in the world will not buy your life back or the time that you have wasted. The most delicate and precious thing you have on this Earth is the limited amount of time you have to make the best of yourself and make a positive impact on other people.

Live your life now. People are often so focused on the future they forget to live in the present. I know I am often guilty of that. "Think selfless, not selfish."

There is truth to the saying "Eat, drink, and be merry, for tomorrow you die." I believe it means, live the life you have now at this moment, because you don't know when you are going to lose it. A word of caution, you must be practical and balanced. Live your life like you love it and your positive affirmations will deliver. But you can't fake being positive, your soul knows the truth. You can't lie to yourself, some part of you will detect the lie. Our time here on Earth is limited, do all you can do and be the best you can be.

I came across this quote, I don't know who wrote it, but it poignantly gives you insight as to the value of time.

"To realize the value of ONE YEAR, ask a student who failed a grade.

To realize the value of ONE MONTH, ask a mother who gave birth to a premature baby.

To realize the value of ONE WEEK, ask the editor of a weekly newspaper.

To realize the value of ONE HOUR, ask the lovers who are waiting to meet.

To realize the value of ONE MINUTE, ask a person who missed the train.

To realize the value of ONE SECOND, ask a person who just avoided an accident.

Treasure every moment! Yesterday is history.

Tomorrow is mystery.

Today is a gift. That's why it's called the present!"

-Anonymous

**FACE YOUR FEARS
AND
FIGHT YOUR FEARS!
DON'T YOU EVER GIVE UP!
THIS IS YOUR LIFE!
YOU DECIDE YOUR OUTCOME!
LIFT YOUR HEAD UP
AND
RISE TO THE OCCASION!**

"Trials, temptations, disappointments -- all these are helps instead of hindrances, if one uses them rightly. They not only test the fiber of a character, but strengthen it. Every conquered temptation represents a new fund of moral energy. Every trial endured and weathered in the right spirit makes a soul nobler and stronger than it was before." - James Buckham

RISE UP AND STEP OUT OF THE BOX!

What does it mean to be inside a mental mind-box? It's being mentally trapped on account of not having expanded your independent mind. It's letting others tell you how to be and act, overpowering you through manipulation and guilt. It's when fear of failure makes you sweep your ideas, whether brilliant or outlandish, back under the rug. It's when every time you want to try something new, your mind builds a wall to barricade you in.

There is freedom found in "the box of life," and it's a box without walls. So many people are held back by fear. Fear is nothing more than a thought.

Fear is meant to hold you back. Fear makes us uncomfortable with trying something "outside the box." We seem to place limitations on ourselves, afraid of both the possible and the impossible. Why is this? In a few words, fear of failure, rejection, and what others might think of us. We need to overcome these mental blocks, busting right through them. As Brendan Francis said, "Many of our fears are tissue paper thin, and a single courageous step would carry us clear through them." Once you develop the habit of overcoming limiting thoughts, you will be on your way to an action-packed life.

I came from a failing background, but once I got past the fear of being a failure as a child, the only way I could go was up. I once heard Dr. Wayne Dyer state "When you change the way you look at things, the things you look at change." How true that is! So what if you have bad habits, lack drive, or have endured a life of tragedy? We need to think of these situations as teachers that aid us in improving our character. Throughout my life, I've taken the opportunity to learn lessons from hard knocks. I wouldn't be writing this book if I never learned, or wasn't able to move along in a forward, positive direction. Even when we have every advantage in this life, we often choose not to advance in a positive direction.

If we look at ourselves as action-takers and winners, we will no longer settle for a life filled with the "Poor Me Syndrome." When we box ourselves in, allow dreams to fade away, or let the world set limits to what we deserve, we become nothing more than robots with no purpose but to breathe in air and do just enough to get by. Most people want to make a difference in both their lives and the lives of other people, but lack a plan of action. Guess what? The plan will not drop onto your lap and say "Here I am!" You have to make the map yourself. It is going to be a crazy maze, but once you have set your purpose and your goal, your map and compass will show you true north, and nobody will ever hold you back again. Today is your day to start a new life. It is all starts with your attitude. Make the best of it, and life will deliver something great to you.

DREAMS GIVE YOU THE WINGS
TO FLY FEARLESSLY AND HAVE PURPOSE

Do you believe that the impossible is possible? Do you believe that what you can think yourself to be, you can become? Do you believe that dreams are meant to become reality? I am here to tell you to believe beyond your dreams. I try to live my life thinking that I don't want to die before I die. I don't want to live life like a zombie. I want to live my life to the fullest. My spirit imitates my imagination. My creativity comes from my imagination. Whatever your simple mind can dream and create, it can do so much more. Believe beyond your dreams!

A question anyone might have is, "How do I overcome limiting thoughts?" Well I am going to go into detail about what I have done in my life, and it all started with a dream. At some point in your life, no doubt, you have had a dream. Maybe it was to be a doctor, an astronaut, professional sports player, a race-car driver, an artist, the President of the United States, or a rock star. Even if you don't have a dream right now, you did when you were a child, because every child dreams. Even as adults, we dream. It may be a dream of getting out of an impoverished area, getting a better job or being rich. Everything is attainable if you focus on what you want and take the action to move towards that goal. Everything is motion, you are either moving forwards or backwards. There is no standing still. When you stand still, you are not moving forward, and if you are not moving forward you are going backwards. Focus on the sky and the stars and not the sewage of the world. Do not mentally starve yourself of living your dreams.

So many people mentally starve themselves as they use their power to help others to achieve their dreams, but then lack the energy and drive to help their own self achieve. The end result is that you are not living for you. You are living for others. The one person you should take care most is you. You have to live with "you" your entire life, so make it great a great journey.

Try to go back in your mind and remember when you were about seven years old, how you felt, how free from the world and responsibilities you were, how you got along with every-one and had love in your heart. Remember how back in the old days there didn't seem to be any worries. Emulate this child you once were, and this child will set your mind free. When your mind is free, you can dream again, taking flight upon the wings that you have been given to use.

As the years pass on, the more serious you become, the more grumpy and stressed out you are. You rarely have time to think about yourself, and opportunities for a good laugh are few and far between. You become a complainer, believing that life is always unfair. I know, I have been there. What has helped me overcome this grumpy old man's attitude is simply becoming like a child, and just being a goofball. Laugh, laugh and laugh! Think about the innocence of children, and how they are rarely depressed. We as adults teach them by example how to become angry, sad, and disappointed. Children are only about love and being happy. But they pick up on adult behaviors, eventually acting out what they see. So be like an innocent, loving, happy and carefree child, before it learns the destructive patterns of this world. Go to a park and watch kids play freely, listen to their laughter, open your heart to their happiness. You are only getting older, but now is the time to rekindle the youth inside of you and begin dreaming the impossible. Even if your dream appears ridiculous, be ridiculous in equal measure by believing in it. Where there is laughter and goofiness, there is also the energy to make dreams come true.

It all starts with energy. Energy creates motion, motion creates action, action creates results, results create achievement, achievement creates self-confidence, and self-confidence creates the mindset that allows you to help others fashion their destiny.

Change the world by changing yourself. Once you are confident about your own ability to achieve, you can help create a world of achievers through your example. People want to be successful and happy. But happiness is rare these days. You can usually spot a happy person because it is so unusual. There are tons of unhappy people who seem uninterested in anything but their own misery. Don't pay them any attention. They will change when they are ready. I heard this saying once: "When the student is ready, the master will appear." It is hard to help someone who doesn't want to help themselves. You can waste a lot of time and energy on people who just don't want to change, because they like the attention they receive when somebody helps them play the victim role.

Stay away from these people. You will eventually lose your own energy, and then you will have two people living in misery together.

You absolutely become a product of your environment. Focus on hanging out with people that laugh a lot and are uplifting. I don't care if they are rich or poor, at least they're happy, and you benefit from plugging your mind into happiness, and avoiding negativity and self-conscious suffering. I have heard motivational speakers who say that in order for you to become rich, you must be involved with the rich, act like the rich, smell like the rich, drive a car like the rich, eat like the rich and dress like the rich. I think you can learn from the rich, but most of all be sure you are being true to yourself, and are in search of a meaningful life. Life is not all about the dollar. Life is about time well spent. Money cannot buy you time. Some of these speakers also say that you shouldn't hang around with poor people, but I am here to tell you that some of the richest people I know are the poorest financially. They are rich in spirit. The accumulation of money does not rule over them, but accumulating the trappings of a meaningful life does.

I have heard some wonderful stories about how kids with cancer and cancer survivors overcame their heartache with family, music, and laughter. They were all in bad situations, and yet they could still put a smile on their face. These are extraordinary people. Anyone that has been through hell and can still put a genuine smile and on their face is a great person. They laugh in the face of adversity. It is absolutely beautiful!

Don't try to fit in and be somebody that you aren't; be true to yourself. Being rich does not mean you are any happier. In fact, it often means more problems. I have had the opportunity to make more money than the average person, and guess what?

I don't believe having money made me any happier. When you have money, you get stressed out whenever your savings account starts to dwindle. You freak out from worry over being broke again. Stress overcomes you, because you want to be back on top and have lots of money again. It's a cycle. Being rich is a state of mind. You can be rich in health and family, whereas another person may not have a healthy body or a family, yet has plenty of money. What would you rather have? Money or health? Money or family? Remember, family is the most important thing. I learned that lesson the hard way, but I am glad that I learned it.

I find that a lot of poor people base their wealth on the amount of time they have, instead of on the material possessions they own. They don't need all the fancy cars, houses, and dinnerware. They are more interested in having time to fish, help others in need, and spend time with their children.

See for yourself how many rich fathers spend time with their kids, or how many rich parents have nannies. They are so busy working and making money that they can't be there for their kids. I guarantee that their children are not their first priority. They themselves are their first priority. Remember, it's about being selfless instead of selfish, especially when it comes to helping your children grow up and become amazing adults. All it takes is the time to do it, and then doing it.

Many people who know me know I have a big personality. I like to laugh and joke around. Sure there are times when I have been completely stressed out on one of my big projects. I'm an owner of a company, it happens. And I often allow myself to suffer instead of getting in touch with my soul, which has the power to calm me by letting the voice of reason speak. To regain that lost contact with my soul, I grab my guitar and start writing about my feelings, and in that way pull myself up out of my own hell. At times like these I have often come up with a great song. You might try working out, playing sports, writing, or doing the yard-work. I love being in the garden. I find peace when I am working with the soil.

That soil was created by the God of this world, and sometimes when you're on your knees, weeding the yard, with nothing between you and the soil, an idea pops into your head and you discover a new way to look at your situation.

Another idea is doing something totally "UnYou." In my case, I call it being UnDerek." Do the opposite of what you would normally do. If you don't play sports, get a basketball, go to a park, and try to shoot some hoop. If you are the type that doesn't like to get your hands dirty, then go get your hands dirty and work in the soil. If you hate to write poems, try writing one and express yourself full-heartedly. If you like rock music, listen to classical music or opera. If you like to drink beer and watch TV all the time, try not drinking and go for a hike. The point is to do something opposite of what you would normally do, something outside the walls of a boxed-in life. Don't limit yourself to just those things that make you comfortable. Live a portion of every day being uncomfortable so that you can grow. Get out of your routine and blaze your own path to greatness.

There is a verse in the Bible describing a particular incident in which the Apostles came to Jesus, saying, "Who is the greatest in the kingdom of Heaven?" And calling to him a child, he put him in the midst of them, and said, "'Truly, I say to you, unless you turn and become like children, you will never enter the kingdom of heaven.'" Matthew 18.1-3, KJV Holy Bible

Dreams are for both young and old alike. Age doesn't matter. What matters is the youthfulness of heart and mind. Why do you think Disneyland is so successful? People want to feel young and dream about the unreal. But what is not real can become real. When this world was created, all that was here was land, water, and the natural resources. Look around you now; everything has been created, from paper to tires to buildings to movies to rocket ships. At one time, all these things were unimaginable. But at some point somebody had a dream, and they followed through with it, and persisted through many disappointments and failed attempts. That's why you have a car to drive, a cell phone, TV and computer. The individuals who invented and created everything you use, from a hairdryer to gasoline, had a dream and nothing would stop them from realizing it.

These innovators had three very important characteristics that helped them push through all the self-imposed barriers: Determination, Perseverance, and Endurance.

To push the boundaries of invention and do the impossible, many of these people had to ignore the negative feedback from friends, family, and critics. And now, despite legions of nay-sayers throughout history, we have used the Earth's resources to become a society filled with miracles. Albert Einstein once said that "there are only two ways to live your life. One is as though nothing is a miracle and the other is as though everything is a miracle." We have the rest of our lives from this moment on to make our dreams happen. Live life from the seat of your imagination, for in the very center of imagination is found the idea of what you most want to be. I can't guarantee how long your life will be, so go for it while you still can. And who knows, maybe one small change in the way you live your life will serve to extend your life. Do not believe what you see, see what you believe.

WILL IT!

There is a four letter word that is woven into the fabric of my soul, and that word is WILL. I have always had the WILL to persevere, the WILL to believe in myself, the WILL to take action and the WILL to never give up. This word has given me the unyielding strength to conquer all the negative situations I've encountered. WILL has allowed me to make something positive out of my life. I came up with an acronym for W.I.L.L., about never giving up. There is always a way! You can do whatever you want to, but you must first have the WILL to follow things all the way through to success.

W-Whatever
I- Is
L- Lacking,
L- Learn!

There are those people who say, "I would have done something with my life if I had more time." Then there are those who say, "I could have been something if I had only applied myself." Or how about the ones who say, "I should have devoted more time to my family." Woulda, Coulda, Shoulda— but most of all, SHOULDA NEVER GIVEN UP!!!! Life is a test, and we have to face reality. Success comes from trying and trying again until finally you succeed. All it takes is a spark and for me that spark starts the flame of desire and the will to never give up!

When I was married at age 23, I didn't even have a job. I got laid off right before the wedding day. In fact, the night before our wedding, my wife's maid of honor called her up very concerned, and told her that she shouldn't marry me because I was immature and didn't have a job. When my wife told me about the phone call that night, I couldn't believe it. My wife sure had a lot of faith in me. Needless to say, it was awkward the next day when looking at the maid of honor.

We stayed our distance, but I guess I can't blame her for what she did. She was just another person who didn't have faith in me. My wife had complete faith in me, why else would you marry an unemployed man. I am here to tell you that we were living off of love. Then my wife was laid off from her job a month after we were married. We were both unemployed, living off unemployment. We were living on noodles and frozen vegetables, with the occasional hotdog thrown in. The honeymoon marriage was short-lived, and now we were in the real world. It was a crazy time for us. We had lots of stress, arguments, and doubts about whether our marriage was even going to work. At one point we thought about calling it quits and going back home to our parents.

But we had a meeting and decided we would be a team from that point on. We had never lived with each other and barely even knew one another. We had only been dating for a few months before I proposed, and we were married just one year from the day we met. It was quite an eventful year. I just knew she was the one for me. When you know, you know. So right after we were married, we were completely broke and living off unemployment. We were having the hardest time getting along and wondering what we were going to do with ourselves. I finally found a job in sales and promised myself that I would never be broke again. With hard work I excelled at my new occupation, but I could never have done it without my wife's support and the WILL within me. I was determined to improve my life, and with that determination I succeed in providing a quality life for my wife and children. Before we had children, I was able to pay for my wife to complete her schooling at a California State University without taking out a student loan. I am proud of her to be so determined to do the schooling and achieve her degree.

There are two words that, when used together, really get under my skin. They are "I can't." Once you say those words, you are right! You have sold yourself out and will give up without a fight.

If you ever get into a situation where you want to give up, you will do much better for yourself by saying "I can do this," "I can make this happen," and, "I can win." Just the words "I can" produce more energy for your mind, and this will empower you. Life is hard, but only the tough-minded will get somewhere. Everything you want in life is within your reach. But you have to empower yourself to reach out and grab it. There is no comfort in being comfortable. Comfort comes from the strength earned from growing through discomfort. Comfort comes by gaining strength from adversity. Comfort is self-confidence. Comfort comes from knowing that you have the WILL to do whatever it takes.

"I've missed over 9,000 shots in my career. I've lost almost 300 games. 26 times I've been trusted to take the game-winning shot...and missed. I've failed over and over and over again in my life. And that is why I succeed." -- Michael Jordan

Do not hesitate to exercise your WILL in order to take the actions necessary to shaping your life the way you want. Remember, this is *your* life, not your parents, teachers', church authorities', neighbors', friends' or boss's. Take control now so that when you are older, you won't let everyone walk all over you and make you subservient. You are equal to any other person, and nobody is better than you. We all have the same blood, we are of the same species, and that means nobody is greater than you. Not me, not the President of the United States. It's all a frame of mind. I have been in the same room with people who are worth five-hundred million dollars, even billions. They are no different and no better than you or I. The only difference between them and the average person is that they took decisive action and "went for it." To make their dreams reality, they persevered through all the hard times until they got to where they are today. That's it! Their great success came from simply following things through to the end.

I designed this "reactionary mind map" that I hope will give you an idea of where you really are today. The big circle is the "Negative Nuclear Self." Surrounding this circle are examples of pressures that may be consuming your mind and overwhelming you. Each dot has another set of pressures, including too much time being taken from you and having doubts. The analysis can then be taken up another notch, and help point out another set of pressures.

By adding pressures upon pressures, and realizing how these pressures add up to create a massive burden, you can finally come to recognize the ways in which your mind continually acts like a broken record. Because you may be constantly trying to dig your way out of a ditch, you come to feel overwhelmed, like you're never accomplishing anything. You find yourself "ping-ponging" through life, lost in the maze of your mind. You go through the routines of life like a zombie, and are zombies happy? Not very.

The second, smaller circle is the one called "What Self Wants To Be." It is directly connected to and impacted by the negative aspects of ourselves. It is correlated with our mind, and our mind feeds us doubts about our ability to accomplish our personal dreams. The negative pressures overwhelm our dreams, making them into a smaller priority than they should be. Doubts trickle into fear and fear leads to a failure to try anything.
So much of our energy is spent dealing with the daily pressures that we may never take the time to do what we want to do, and that is accomplishing our dreams.

Use your WILL. We all have it somewhere buried in our hearts. To me WILL is the "Holy Grail" of building the life you've always wanted. It separates the achievers and those so-called "dreamers" who are unwilling to take action.

If you lack the WILL, you get the leftovers of what life has to offer. Go out into this world of limitless possibilities and make WILL your best friend!

PROCRASTINATE?
OR
PRO-ACTIVATE?

Here are a few things to consider when evaluating your current way of thinking and the life you're now living. Ask yourself these questions

Am I self-sufficient?

Do I thrive or simply survive?

Does unbalance control me or do I control my balance?

Does time control me or do I control my time?

Does money control me or do I control my money?

Does food control me or do I control my food?

Does anger control me or do I control my anger?

Does passion control me or do I control my passion?

Do I try to find the humor in the things I do, or do I take things too seriously?

Do I let my body be a source of positive energy, or do I let it become a source of negativity?

Does sleep control me or do I control my sleep?

Do I live life to the fullest or do I live life with no fullness?

Don't let this life pass you by.   This is the most important lesson to take from this chapter.   Don't wait to live life and then lay there on your deathbed having regrets about not having done what you always wanted to do. Consider your future self, and ask if this person regrets having never taken the time, or if they didn't have the guts to go for it. The cemetery will always be there. And a person doesn't have to be deceased to live in a graveyard. It just depends on whether you let yourself die before you've even died. You can take the safe and boring way, but this way guarantees that you will one day have regrets.

Better to live life the exciting life full of curiosity and opportunity. Either way you're going to end up in the cemetery, so why not live before you die?

Procrastinate or proactivate? This is one of the most important questions you will ever ask yourself. The way you answer this question will determine your destiny. It's that simple. Let me make it even simpler: you have two choices in life, TO DO, or TO NOT DO. The great thing about your life is that you alone have the power to decide. You decide your outcome through your actions. When you're debating between doing and not doing, it will be your actions that finally decide the matter.

So what holds people back from taking action? I believe it is fear of being uncomfortable and the fear of failure. I find it hard to believe that it's the fear of success, as I have often heard people say. We all want success and a better life, but some people aren't willing to make the effort required to achieve it. Settling for procrastination will make you a prisoner in your own world. This world is full of miracles, and there are endless possibilities. Depending on your outlook on life, you can either thrive in it or die in it. To thrive, you must have the passion for action.

Love what you do. You should love your job, and if you don't, find a job that you do love. If you love it, you will excel at it. You spend the majority of your day working. You might as well love what you do.

I believe procrastination is a major cause of sadness, depression, suicide, and financial despair. I have seen people imprisoned by depression. The depression takes over their whole mind and body, much like a disease. Sometimes it takes months to pull themselves out. Procrastination causes depression because when people procrastinate they allow things to pile up higher and higher, never taking the time to clear their mind of all the clutter. It becomes overwhelming, and soon it becomes too much work. Everything you've put off catches up to you at some point, and then you just burn out. Remember, procrastination is the ultimate thief of your time. I believe firmly in "not putting off until tomorrow what I can do today."

Chances are that if you procrastinate in one aspect of your life, such as business, you will also procrastinate in your personal life. You must live your life with urgency in order to accomplish your dreams. You should never forget about the present day and the moment you find yourself in, because it is all these tiny moments put together that determine the sum of your future. Every moment provides you with an opportunity to work toward a future that will profit you mentally, spiritually, and financially.

Remember the parable of the talents in the Bible. I believe the word "talent" can in this parable be interpreted as meaning both money and an ability—literally, a "talent" we might have.

"A man, going on a journey, summoned his slaves and entrusted his property to them. To one he gave five talents; to another he gave two; to another he gave one, to each according to his ability. Then he went away. The one who had received the five talents went off at once and traded with them, and made five more talents. In the same way, the one who had the two talents made two more talents. But the one who had received the one talent went off and dug a hole in the ground and hid his master's money.

"After a long time the master of those slaves came and settled accounts with them. Then the one who had received the five talents came forward, bringing five more talents, saying, "Master, you handed over to me five talents; see, I have made five more talents." His master said to him, "Well done, good and trustworthy slave; you have been trustworthy in a few things, I will put you in charge of many things; enter into the joy of your master." And the one with the two talents also came forward, saying, "Master, you handed over to me two talents; see, I have made two more talents." His master said to him, "Well done, good and trustworthy slave; you have been trustworthy in a few things, I will put you in charge of many things; enter into the joy of your master." Then the one who had received the one talent also came forward, saying, "Master, I knew that you were a harsh man, reaping where you did not sow, and gathering where you did not scatter seed; so I was afraid, and I went and hid your talent in the ground. Here you have what is yours."

"His master replied, "You wicked and lazy slave! You

knew, did you, that I reap where I did not sow, and gather where I did not scatter? Then you ought to have invested my money with the bankers, and on my return I would have received what was my own with interest. So take the talent from him, and give it to the one with the ten talents. For to all those who have, more will be given, and they will have an abundance; but from those who have nothing, even what they have will be taken away. As for this worthless slave, throw him into the outer darkness, where there will be weeping and gnashing of teeth." Matthew 25: 14-30 KJV

What I take from this parable is the lesson that it doesn't matter how much we have been given, what matters is what we do with what has been given. We are the masters over our mind and actions. We must do rather than wait. The servants who were rewarded had faith enough to make something more out of what they'd been given. It is interesting that the master says "you wicked and lazy slave."

I know from experience that even after having worked my butt off, I sometimes got nowhere. This might translate into a loss of money and time. I wonder what would have happened if one of the servants had showed a loss, which might technically have been considered worse than the zero-sum gain of the servant who buried his talent. If I had to operate and show results within a specific time-frame, I would have had to claim a loss, and what would the master have done with me? Would he have penalized me for failing, or would he reward me for trying? I like to think that the master would have at least acknowledged a worthy effort, even if it did end up in failure.

I think this parable illustrates why people procrastinate. If they try, they might fail, and because they care about the image people have of them, the possibility of failure makes action too risky. I say screw the image and screw what other's think about you. Let actions speak for themselves. You should never give up on what you want. You never fail until you stop trying. Try, try and try. Anyone who ridicules or pokes fun at a person who is trying is the real "loser."

Something this parable didn't discuss is using one's talents to help others, being selfless instead of selfish. I wonder what the outcome would have been had one of the servants told his master that he gave his money away to the poor and needy, to bring them happiness and give them hope. I would consider it selfless and generous. Wouldn't this be noble too? Maybe more so than making money for the master. We shouldn't be selfish, always thinking "What can I get out it?" or, "What's in it for me?" Being generous and giving to people has helped me become a more tender and "real" man, not to mention richer in spirit. Moreover, there have been times in my life when I needed help. How can I accept help in good faith if I am unwilling to help others?

Do you know what the opposite of faith is? It is Fear. Faith and conviction in your actions is like food for your passion. It's hard to achieve positive results in any endeavor without faith and conviction. Doubt is what drives the final nails into our coffins. Remember, it's all in the way you look at things. Keep a positive attitude, stay focused, take action and anticipate the reaction.

Test yourself. Look at your bank account and see how it makes you feel. Or get on the scale and see how much you weigh; are you happy with what it says? Now visualize the results you want. We all know these results are attainable because we see people everyday who have attained their desired results. It's not hard knowing what to do, because we all know what to do. The challenge is to do what we know we ought to. It's that simple. Focus on breaking it down to baby steps, because baby steps are motion, and motion makes things happen.

With every action you take there is a guaranteed reaction. Life renews everyday. Engage life, and it will engage you. Let us make the best of our lives!

"Time is more valuable than money. You can get more money, but you cannot get more time." **Jim Rohn**

FATHER TO SON, TIME WELL SPENT. FAMILY ALWAYS COMES FIRST!

Recently I had one of the most amazing life-changing experiences I've ever had. I want to share it with you because there was a part of me that was healed by it. It was a Saturday morning and my wife had just left to go shopping. My six year-old son was complaining about not having some toy that his friend had. He was starting to cry because Mom was not going to buy it for him while she was out shopping. He was getting very frustrated. I told him, "Son, don't worry about it, we are so fortunate to have what we have." He didn't appreciate that comment and when I asked him to pick up his coat, he stood there defiantly. I then said in a commanding, fatherly voice, "You had better have an attitude of gratitude." He ran to the couch, hid his head and started crying hysterically. I realized that yelling at him was not going to help him to stop throwing his fit.

I was standing in the kitchen and said, "Son, come here." He came, and I bent down to his eye level and said in a very loving voice, "It's all about having an attitude of gratitude. Did you know that when I was your age, I didn't even own a toothbrush or a bicycle. You are so fortunate to have those things. When I was your age, I didn't even a have a Mom or Dad who cared about me or loved me. I didn't have a real home or family to stay with." His amazed eyes just stared up at me, and for a moment I think he understood exactly what I was saying. I then said, "No matter what, before toys and friends, family comes first and I want you to know that I love you very much." I put my hand over my heart and said it again with tears starting to flow down my face. "I love you so much, son. When I was your age nobody ever told me that, and I want you to know I love you with all of my heart." My tears were flowing and my voice was trembling as I said those words. I wanted to make sure that he knew what a heart full of love felt like.

As I tearfully conveyed my love for the third time, I saw tears flowing from his eyes and he ran to me and gave me a hug. At that moment our hearts were pounding right next to each other. We were silent as we held each other, which made our hearts pounding seem all the louder. My mind wasn't anywhere but right there in that moment, feeling the love my son had for me. I held him in my arms, embracing him in pure love. I cried with him and told him how proud of him I was, that he was a great son and a great sibling to his brother and sister. I continued to tell him about the hard times I had had as a six year-old, a little boy who nobody wanted, and reminded him that he was so very lucky to have a Mom and Dad that love him with all of their souls. I picked him up and brought him to the couch and just held him in my arms like he was a brand new baby again. I held him for half an hour, just staring into his eyes and telling him how much I loved him and how lucky I was to have him as a son. I told him that he makes me appreciate life every day, and how he sets a great example for me. He was so in tune with my emotions, and it gave me a sense of closure and security. I gave him the love that was never given to me as a child his age. It amazed me that I was talking to him and loving him as if I were his age, wishing that someone had talked to me and held me like that. It was a very surreal experience.

I love all of my children with all my heart. They are so very precious. My 6 year old son is such a loving, detailed and thoughtful little man. My 5 year old son shows so much affection and is in tune with others feelings. My 2 year old daughter is just a little princess that is so girly and so thoughtful. She is such a little helper. I love spending time with them, watching them grow and watching their minds develop and problem-solve. Do you remember the great memories of being a kid? We were all kids at one time. I invite you to close your eyes right now and think about some of the funniest memories of your childhood. Maybe it was building a fort, camping or jumping in the lake, fishing or dressing up like a princess. Think about the greatest times you had with your Mom, Dad and family. Maybe it was helping your Mom bake cookies, or piggy-back rides on your Dad, or wrestling with him or playing catch. Maybe it was just having your mother hold you, giving you that awesome motherly love. Maybe it was just going for a drive with Dad on an errand, and you were just happy hanging out with him.

It took me a while in fatherhood to realize that families should always come first. I was guilty of putting work, friends and hobbies before family. I have my wife to thank for helping me see the light. Children are unbelievable creations. I have seen friends whose work, church and friends come first. The cell phone is also a major distraction when you're having family time. I found that out. When we are with physically with our families, our minds should be completely with them too. Just like the old days. There never was a cell phone conversation to break up family time. I believe the family unit was a lot stronger back then than it is now. So many distractions are tearing down the family.

My foster family was probably one of the last families in America to get a microwave oven. My foster Mom felt that the microwave would destroy the family because it would no longer make eating dinner together a priority. In the past, if you came home late for dinner it would be cold, and you'd it make it a priority to get to dinner on time in order to have a warm meal. Thanks to the microwave you can now always reheat your food. We can learn a lot from our parents and grandparents.

I grew up in a religion that called for its members to devote a lot of extra time to volunteer church service. Some people donated all their extra time. Parents would take their free time to complete their duties to the church. I never liked the idea of being away from family. Sometimes their church job was helping out with the youth programs, as often as two times a week, while their young children were at home. Parents were spending time with children not their own, kids whose parents then got a night off. I always thought youth leaders should have been those with older children, instead of those who had babies and toddlers. It's not fair that a person with children under the age of five has to spend time with other parents' children. These parents are being robbed of precious time with their own kids. People with small children sometimes give all of their free time to a church in the name of God. But I think this is completely wrong. God isn't always about church. Personally, I am more prone to look for God in the miracle of my family.

Little miracles can happen in your home everyday. Godliness can be in your home all the time. I sometimes feel that my home is more Godly than a church. If I put family first, I'll always feel gratitude to God. Even with all the religions and churches teaching us love and tolerance, there seems to be a growth of hate, anger, dishonesty, violence and disrespect amongst people in this world. Parents' example of pure, unconditional love shows our children that real love is better than religious creeds. Live by example. Love is nurtured in the home. If we want a world full of love, we have to recognize that it all starts with the family. Others say they're focusing on their religious duties because God wants them to. I believe God wants you to be home with your families. Some may call their duties to church "building the Kingdom of God," but build the Kingdom of God in your home first.

I have heard the saying that "my church congregation is like another family." That helps make people who don't have a family feel great about going to church. That is a great feeling of security to know that someone else cares about you. But those of us who do have a family are better served by being home during the week and doing something together as a family. Don't you think that is what God wants? Families first? God allows us to create families through the power of procreation. Isn't that Godly to create a family?

Let me give you an example of time misspent. The mother is home with the kids, the husband works forty to fifty hours a week, plus commuting, gets home late, eats dinner in a rush without being part of the family, says hello and may talk to his kids for about fifteen minutes, and is then off to church helping raise somebody else's kids. Then they may have to do a youth activity or meetings on Saturday, then it's church on Sunday and meetings possibly again. So when does this father spend time with his own kids, instead of getting wrapped up in assignments and responsibilities? But who really gains here? The church. Tell me who suffers here? The family, wife and eventually the husband with all his duties. Sooner or later, when his kids grow up, he may realize that he didn't spend enough time with his kids or build a strong relationship with them, justifying it as what God wanted of him. In the end, we don't know when his life will be over. And the question is, how will he be remembered? A great church member or a great dad? It is hard, but we must all strive to have a healthy balance and show our families that they come first. Help your family first, then help others! Here is a thought. Instead of building a church, build a home where your own family is centered on God? It doesn't take a fancy meeting place to bring God in. Your home can be your own temple. It doesn't cost anything, and you are literally building your own Heaven on Earth. Your family may live in this Kingdom of Heaven for years to come, with each generation building a new part of it. We created our son's and daughter's through God's power of procreation. Heaven can be in our home, free ourselves of all the distractions from the outside world pulling us away from our beautiful heavenly family, and rid ourselves of manipulation by others for their own agenda. Our agenda should be about what is real, and that is to have a balanced family life.

TRIUMPHS!
HOW A LITTLE FOSTER KID GREW UP
AND TOUCHED PEOPLE'S LIVES.

Who would have thought that a little foster kid who was given up on, diagnosed with retardation, learning disabilities, anger issues, and withdrawal from reality, could one day grow up to touch so many people? The following comments are just a fraction of the numerous emails and letters I have received. It is very humbling to have people write such nice things about me. They strengthen me and give me hope for a better tomorrow. They make me feel as if my life were on the right course. The first few comments are from a U.S. Marine Platoon stationed in Iraq. They heard my songs and wrote me some very wonderful comments about them. What is amazing is that most of this platoon never knew their Mom or Dad, and grew up in group homes or orphanages. They lived a life similar to mine. Take a read and share some tears with some of these great men and women.

KONG: Derek, my favorite song of yours is "Goodnight Soldier." I grew up a foster child like you. To me, my heroes are military Moms everywhere. If they only knew how much their sons and daughters in Iraq think of them, miss them, love them, and risk all to protect them and their future, I think they probably would feel so filled with pride that they would float away like birthday balloons up to the ceiling of the ballroom. I never knew my birth Mom or Dad, but I have been really fortunate while here, along with our entire platoon to be "adopted" by a beautiful lady stateside who allows our platoon to call her Mom. Semper Fi Moms everywhere! "Goodnight Soldier" always makes me think of the military Moms everywhere, worrying about us all. It's an awesome song.

DOC EAGLE: Derek, your CD, *Goodnight Soldier* is entirely first rate. It's a platoon favorite. I like your music because your themes are real. This might sound strange, but your song " I Wanna Be A Kid" reminds me so much of my wife because of the time I told her about my sordid life tale of being a foster child. My wife was my hero. She was a nurse and she was always there for every soldier who ever needed a caring, compassionate goddess in their hour of pain. She was the kindest soul that God ever sent down from Heaven. Her smile was like the rainbow after a Virginia thunderstorm, her voice was that of an angel. Our first date, she listened to the story of my harsh childhood. I knew I was in love with her, and was hooked and did ***not*** want to be hooked—damn, I never had anyone reach out or love me when I was a child or a young adult—and it felt messed up to be loved. That is how messed up I was at the time. So I thought I would tell her my most horrible secret and by doing that she would then run for the hills and I would not have to be in love with her. She did not run for the hills, she just took my hand gently and said, ***Doc,***

192

that is the past. It was the best advice anyone ever gave to me. Her eyes were like two Hawaiian turquoise pools, I fell in them and no longer cared that I had fallen in love. I loved her so much I just would have died in her place on 9/11, had God asked me or given me the opportunity. That the Gentleman upstairs did not give me the opportunity to save my wife with my own life is a bone of contention I plan on discussing when I am called back to the eternal homeland. In the meantime, I try to do the right thing here on Earth until it's time to go home for dinner with my wife up in Heaven. I cannot count the times I have listened to your song "I Just Wanna Be A Kid." I want to tell you how it really helped me with my pain, both of childhood and with the loss of my wife. The child spirit is really in that song, it tells a good story, but it also gives hope. Keep on writing that awesome music.

CHERRY: Derek, I like your music because to me, the kind of music you write is the kind that touches the soul deep. Your music makes me feel closer to God. God is my hero. He has somehow kept me alive and *keeping on keeping on* all these years, through a real harsh childhood in foster care and times prior to joining the Marines when I really did not think I would make it to adulthood. I think God sent the music to you, and it is beautiful you can share your talent with the world. God is always there for me, and has brought so many great people into my life; these jar buddies of mine, Sally, Danny, and just about the best friend I could ask for, War Dawg. He brought me to the US Marines, and they turned a sad young man into a Marine with goals, positive attitude, and honor, courage and commitment. Semper Fi, God! So when I listen to your music, that is what I am reminded of, all that is good in the world.

TEX: Dang-a-lang, Derek, your music is awesome. I grew up in foster care, and never had a Mom figure in my life. And then I came to Iraq as a Marine and met up with WAR DAWG. One day I was sitting around feeling sorry for myself. It was my birthday and no one really knew or gave a damn. My team leader, War Dawg came up and said, WASSUP TEX? I was so bummed I just shrugged. She said, CHEER UP DUDE, I HAVE THIS GREAT CD I AM GONG TO PLAY FOR YOU. War Dawg played your *Goodnight Soldier* CD, the track called "I JUST WANNA BE A KID." Dang that music just loosened the knot in my heart big time. The words of it really got me, and before I knew it I was telling War Dawg about my bad times as a kid. Forever your song will be the symbol of how I got that chip off my shoulder, and made me realize I had a platoon Mom, War Dawg. War Dawg is always going to be my best friend, and listening to that song of yours was the moment I knew it. ***Damn Real***. War Dawg is my hero cause she is the only person who can out-shoot me on SAW, is not afraid to ride in the hot seat. She can make me laugh all the time, she puts up with my craziness. She is the best leader a jar could get. I would follow her into battle anywhere with buck-ass nothing if need be. She likes dogs like I do, she never gets grossed out by anything we say, and she can pick hella good scorpions for our gladiator fights. Lets see what else, she always lets me have her peanut butter crackers out of her MRE's. Plus she is the only one that likes Derek Clarke CDs as much as I do. Plus she will pick up a camel spider with her bare hands. Oh yeah, and she is really Momly. And she can run as fast as me. Lets see, what else, uh, oh yeah she can whup me in Kbar tosses and when everyone falls asleep from me talking she is the only one who will still talk to me and stay awake. Oh yeah, and we both like peppermints and peppermint Tic Tacs. Plus she is really good at video games. Not that we get to play them at this ratty ass FOB. Plus we both like the song "I JUST WANNA FLY," and both think it's the best song ever written. Thanks Derek!

SPIDER: Derek I like your music because it really describes what it is like to feel things deep and not be able to tell anyone. I had a pretty bad childhood. HOW BAD WAS IT SPIDER? Ha ha, it was so bad the orphanage attendants from hell made my DI [drill instructor] at boot camp look like Elvis's doting mama. So being used to abuse, I totally bonded with my DI. Actually he was a good guy. When I was about to give up on a lot of the things, like the weapons training [I had to qualify to be a Marine with corrected vision, these dang coke-bottle glasses would scare off even Bin Laden!—that's why the Marines really took me in, plus they can bounce EMP bombs off my lens to any target just by having Kong swivel my head around….] my DI facilitated me to realize I could do it, and I actually qualified as Expert, when I was worried I would get the boot out of boot. I have a lot of other heroes, but my DI is always going to be my first hero, he was like a Dad, a Big Brother, and a Best Friend all in one. And when I listen to your song "I Just Wanna Be a Kid,"—to me the emotion of that song describes to perfection the feeling I had when I broke through the past into the present positive state of being a US Marine. Thanks Derek, for writing that song. Good luck with your book as well. Semper Fi!

ORLEANS: Hi Derek. I think your music is awesome. My favorite song is "Goodnight Soldier," with fast second I JUST WANNA BE A KID. I asked our Chaplain if I could play your song I JUST WANNA BE A KID when I got baptized over here. Our Chaplain is really funny, and never loses his cool. Picture this dude—this was my baptism: I JUST WANNA BE A KID is blasting out of the boom box held by one of my platoon buddies, turned up on like 90,000 decibels. Just as the Chaplain is baptizing me in the Gulf, a mortar landed in the water like about 25 feet from us and he just laughs and says ***ORLEANS WE ARE BOTH GETTING BAPTISED TODAY…THAT SONG IS REALLY RIGHTEOUS YOU PICKED TO PLAY—WHAT IS IT?*** right before the concussion in the water hit us and knocked us up on the beach like a couple of beach balls. But a miracle happened, the boom box playing your song did not get wet and there you were, still singing your heart out I JUST WANNA BE A KID! Our Chaplain is so cool. He knows just about everything about the Bible, and he is a good role model, he loves his wife and kids and his wife is his most important person and best friend in life. If I did not like being a Marine so much I would be a Chaplain. Well the Chaplain said your song is one of the most spiritual pieces of music he ever heard, cause it's from the heart. And damn real man, I feel the same way. Semper Fi, God Bless you and your family, and hang tough with your book, it will happen.

BRAINIAC: Hi Derek I wanted to tell you how much I appreciate your music. That's a given, straight up. I could tell you why I like your music because I grew up in foster care, but it might just be a rehash of what everyone else is writing up for you. So I will tell you about another fan you have here in Iraq, my personal hero, our little six-year-old Iraqi bud Ahmed. Ahmed is a little dude who we rescued from a fate worse than death, terrorists had kidnapped him, and a couple of them were child molesters. Damn, when we busted in, we caught the bad guy's right in the act of having their kicks with the kids! It was the hardest moment of my life because I wanted to just shoot the heads off all those perverts. Anyone who would hurt a kid man, they are sick. One of the little dudes we rescued was named Ahmed.

I am in awe of Ahmed, because he lived through a real hellish experience and it took him awhile to come out of the shock, but over the past few months he has come back to being a bright, sunny, good kid. He calls me 'Brainman' cause he can't say Brainiac in English. He always gives me High Fives when we go to visit him and check up on him, and tells me he wants to be a Marine just like me when he grows up. He is a cool little dude. Really smart too, we have been teaching him English from comics our adopted military Mom sends us, and he can already read half the words on his own. I always save any Almond M&Ms I get for him; he is a total day-of-the-dead vampire for Almond M&M's. When we brought the kid bags for him and the other children [little cloth bags with handles one of our platoon's ex-girlfriend made and filled for the kids with coloring books, crayons, school stuff, toys, t-shirts, etc.] he said, I WOULD BE HONORED BRAINMAN IF YOU

WOULD CHOOSE MY BAG, in Arabic, and War Dawg translated for me. I really had some major waterworks I had to fight back when the munchkin said that. And then he whispers real cute, BRAINMAN, PLAY THAT DERAQI [How he says Derek] CD—I WANT FLY LIKE MANY CHILDREN. He meant your song "I Just Wanna Be A Kid" on your Goodnight Soldier CD we play for the kids every time we come to visit. When I heard that little dude try to say the name of your song, it really hit me in the heart, the power of your music. Keep on doing what you are doing Derek, it's awesome. Anyway, little Ahmed, he is doing fine. When we were told we were going to write down what your music meant to us, we told little Ahmed, and he says to tell you: DERAQI MUCH MORE MUSIC THAT IS BEAUTIFUL FOR INSIDE.

FORREST G: Hi Derek your music is the bomb. I would just like to tell you I will never forget your song Goodnight Soldier. It's because I grew up in Foster Care and never had anyone really listen to me until I met War Dawg and she was my team leader. The first time I met her she was playing your song, Goodnight Soldier in the office. When I heard that song, I just had to sit down and chill, it was so beautiful a song. War Dawg taught me just about everything I did not know, and I know she knows lots more and will teach me lots more. War Dawg is my hero because no matter how many stupid questions any of us dumb jars ask her, she never makes us feel dumb and she is very patient all the time with us. She really listens when we talk to her, whether one on one or in the team meetings. War Dawg says we are all equals, and she calls us her Jedi Knights or Knights of the Round Table and everybody really feels like that—cause she always gives credit to what we have to say. She is my hero too because she is pure courage on two legs, she is funny, always making us laugh, and she is also "Momly" to us, she always knows what to say when times are hard, like when we lost Stryker.

She is also not afraid of anything and she can shoot an M16 and SAW better than me or Tex. She is my best friend ever. And so when I listen to your song Goodnight Soldier, this is all the stuff I think about, and your song makes me feel all is worthwhile in the world, because your music is so beautiful.

FU MANCHU:. War Dawg told us you had a foster care childhood like all of us. Man when I heard that song I JUST WANNA BE A KID, especially the part where you sing from your kid-self perspective and man, the pain is just there. I totally related to that. I always missed having a Mom, even more than having a Dad. I would listen to the other lucky bastards at my schools complaining about their mothers and really dude I just wanted to rip their hearts out. DAMMIT YOU **HAVE** A MOM, SHUT UP!!!--*is what I wanted to scream.* So your song always makes me think of the importance of a Mother. Because damn real if you don't have one you know how important a Mother is. I like your song, because it also reminds me of my team leader War Dawg. She is my hero because she is an excellent Mother. She raised four sons to be US Marines and even got a letter from her son's DI's saying in all their time in the Corps, they never saw a mother support her sons through boot camp like War Dawg did. This one DI wrote that the motivational letters War Dawg wrote to her son were so good he read them to their entire platoon. ***When I was in boot camp I did not get one single letter, no moto ever, unless I did it myself.*** Damn I bet you can relate to that feeling of being totally alone, because War Dawg told us you grew up similar. If I ever could know my birth Mom I would want her to be just like War Dawg. And she is the one that turned me on to your music. So to me your song will always be a huge thing and these are all the thoughts that go through my mind when I listen to it over and over again. Keep on writing such great music Derek, and God Bless.

FANGBOY: Yo Derek! Your music is the best. I just want to tell you that my favorite song is I JUST WANNA BE A KID. And why it is my favorite? It is my favorite because it always reminds me of my best friend Munch. Munch was my best friend when I was in the orphanage. That little dude had heart. He was born with a condition where he had a normal head but his body was the size of a toddler. He took a total rash from everybody who crossed his path every day of his life. But he was like a lion, man he could roar better than me, who was like gigantic. I met him when we were eight and we were best friends until he died when he was 16 from heart problems relating to his birth condition of being tiny. How we met was it was my first day at the home, and these bigger kids were ready to grind my face into the brick wall.

Munch sped up in his electric wheelchair—knocked down the three bullies like dominos, rode over one of the bullies butt, and then yelled, LEAVE THE KID ALONE OR I WILL PERSONALLY RIP ALL YOU GUYS APART. Damn real, I did not know whether to laugh or pee my pants, but the three bigger kids knew how to react, they booked to the border. And I don't mean the Taco Bell Border man. Munch looks at me and says, "If you are gonna survive in this dung hole you better learn to kick some butt." And we just kind of smiled at each other and were friends from that moment on. Munch's favorite band was Red Hot Chili Peppers, and his only interest was girls. Formidable dude, he would get more girls to dance with him anywhere, anytime than Brad Pitt probably could. And he could spin that wheelchair better than Michael Jackson could moonwalk. Every day I miss him. He had heart. To me, your song, I JUST WANNA BE A KID is like an anthem to Munch. Every time I listen to that song, I do cry, and think of him being free from his body that held him prisoner. He would love that song if he heard it too. What you write about, the pain, overcoming it, that was Munch every day of his life. What you do is awesome, hope you keep on doing it Derek. Thanks and Semper Fi.

BIG DADDY: Derek I am going to tell you my story so you will know how much your song I JUST WANT TO BE A KID means to me. My 'escape' happened when I was ten years old back in Mississippi. I had nine little brothers and sisters. My mama died when I was born, I never knew her. My daddy was a sharecropper, we was dirt poor, never even had shoes for school, except in the winter. He had a "second woman" as they called her. She was as mean as Godzilla and from her all my little sisters and brothers were born, she was even carrying my Dad's kid when my Mom died my Granny said. The platoon says my story sounds like the old school DVD Grapes of

201

Wrath, well damn real it's not far off. They were funning me about my story until I pulled up my shirt and showed them all the scars from the whuppins I used to get. They thought the scars were always from schrap wounds I got here, but Doc Eagle set them straight, he said, "Dudes these were not schrap wounds," because no one would believe I got the scars as a kid.

But anybody who took beatings as a child, they would know they are from my Dad's and Stepmama's whippins. I took 'em for the other kids as well. I didn't want the little ones to get that—thought I might as well get it all, save them the pain. So I stood in their place.

Well one day I went to school, I passed out. I had not eaten any kind of full meal in about a week cause we kids was always short on food and I'd been giving my share to my little sister, Liza.
I had just been given a fresh beating the night before, so blood had seeped through my school shirt. The teacher took me to see the nurse—and she freaked out big time and blew the whistle on my Dad and Stepmama.

Well let me tell ya Derek, I did not want to go home that day. I knew the nurse was sending the sheriff and the county worker out to nail my Dad and Stepmama. I walked home like a zombie that day, knowing I was in for the worst beating of my life when my Dad got that visit from the social. I got home, the three littlest ones, Kara, Sue and Jimmie were all drenched in pee and poop, starving and screaming their heads off, all covered in baby snot. Liza, Cherie, Jamie, Tommy, Donnie and Mikey were all starving as well—trying to do their school books, but so hungry they cold hardly sit up. No food any wheres in the shack, not even a crust of bread. Only good part was no Dad or Stepmama, so no more whippins. I was in no hurry to get the next beatin' when they found out that Nurse had a problem with my back and was sending the social around.

I just sat down, and cried. I ain't ashamed to admit it. I bawled like the babies. I was so tired, so hungry and so scared.

Just then there was a big banging knock on the door. I opened it and there on the step was the Sheriff. He saw the state of us and called the county worker to get over fast. By nightfall we were all in the county orphanage. My Daddy had a friend who worked in the school office, so she called and tipped off my Stepmama—and she went down to warn my Daddy at work what happened and that the Sheriff would be coming by.

My Daddy and Stepmama were never found again—they just took off!

I don't think of my Daddy. But I think of all my brothers and sisters. Within fifteen months at the orphanage they had all been adopted out, the records sealed. They were good lookin' kids. I am glad for em all. I don't know where they all are today, haven't seen em since they all left the orphanage. But I pray God's looked out for em. I guess nobody wanted to adopt a boy with all the scars I had, so I was raised all my life at the orphanage, then went straight into the Marines at eighteen.

Well I will never forget my little brothers and sisters. I like kids so much these Iraqi kids just tear my heart out—they are so cute—the good ones who haven't been taught to hate and kill like old men.

Someday I hope to have my own kids, a big family, that's if my future wife okays that—cause it will be her that does the greatest sacrifice to bring them in the world. What a mom does, a good mom, is huge—way huger than the part any Daddy puts in.

Long story comes to an end Derek—I was really protective of the little kids at the orphanage, they all called me Daddy! The minister and his wife that ran the orphanage started calling me Big Daddy to be funnin'. One of the little orphans I grew up with went into the Marines same time as me, and he called me Big Daddy and it became my jar name in my boot camp platoon.

When I hears that song of yours, I JUST WANNA BE A KID for the first time, it was like something burst inside me, like a balloon with too much water. I just cried for about five minutes. That song you wrote said it all for all the pent up emotions and hell I went through in the first part of my childhood. After I cried I felt 100% better and War Dawg just held me like a little boy till I got through the crying. That is the best song I have ever heard, and the best song I will ever hear, and thanks for writing it. When I listen to it now, I don't feel sad anymore, now it just reminds me of all the good things to come in the future, and how far I got down the road so far in a positive way.

TANK: My favorite song is by Derek Clark and its called Never Give Up. When War Dawg played that CD of Derek Clarke's and I heard that song, my heart, something just came up from the depths of it, and I had to just cry at the end of it. That song is about my life, I said, when I heard it; because life was a real struggle for me. If the Marines had not taken me under their wing, I would definitely be dead by now. The Marines gave me a life; a career, self-respect—and it would have never happened if I had given up. Derek Clarke's song is all about that. Anyone who had a struggle and overcame it would like that song.

ICEMAN: Hola Derek, thanks for doing what you do. My favorite song is I JUST WANNA BE A KID. Because that song is like my life story measured out in pain.

I would be dead by now if Mike, a police officer who befriended me when I was fourteen had not come into my life. Up to that point I had no male role models worth anything. I was a total fool, and running with a bad crew, all older kids and dropouts, and if it had not been for Mike I probably would be in San Quentin waiting for Johnny Cash's second coming instead of being lucky enough to be a US Marine and on this program. This crew I was with, they told me I was supposed to go in this 7/11 and rip off beer to stay in the gang.

Well I go in to do it like an idiot, and Officer Mike pulls up in his squad car with his canine partner, and comes in for his Big Gulp and lard pill or whatever. I got the booze stuck in my skinny a-- pants, oh yeah I was a real bad dude. I start booking past Officer Mike all cool, and he lets me get out of the store. Well crap I get out there, my homies all drove off! Officer Mike says, CAN I TALK TO YOU? He said, YOU LOOK LIKE A SMART GUY. YOU ARE TOO SMART TO BE DOING THIS STUFF. GIVE ME WHAT YOU TOOK I WILL STRAIGHTEN IT OUT THIS TIME. BUT DON'T YOU EVER BE OUT STEALING AGAIN! I freaked out, handed him the 40 ouncer of Budweiser, promised to not do it again. He did not skip a beat dude, he just takes out one of his cards, writes his home number on the back. He said, ask your folks if you can meet me for lunch at the McDonald's and then I will take you over to sign you up for PAL. We need some good football players…You play football son? I don't know what happened, but I just started crying. No one had ever really cared about me before. I told him I was an orphanage kid, the whole nasty history of my crappy life and abusive druggy parents who dumped me there. He did not even blink. He just says, THAT WAS THEN, THIS IS NOW…want a big Gulp? Wait here. Then he straightens it out with the 7/11 guy about the beer, returns it, comes out with a Big Gulp, Cheetos, a cheeseburger and a candy bar for me. He says, the 7/11 guy is cool as long as he knows you are sorry…oh yeah, by the way I got you a job in there, he needs help, it pays minimum wage and you can work M-F afternoons after school, so show up here tomorrow, got that, now want to ride with my partner and me and talk some more? He says. I get in the car, and his partner is like the coolest dog I ever met. Mike goes, This is Officer Lord Jim. That was the dog's name. So we rode around till his shift was over, hella cool, and then he took me home to meet his wife and kids, his wife Cindy was as nice as him and invited me to dinner and then called the orphanage to say I was in a police athletic meeting and Officer Mike would bring me back by curfew. After that I had a friend for life and that is why Officer Mike will always be the part of your song where you sing I JUST WANNA BE A KID. He and his wife even showed up at my boot grad, and I had no one else there so it was especially cool. So this is what goes through my head every time I hear your song I JUST WANNA BE A KID. You are an awesome person and talent Derek, War Dawg has told us a lot about you, and I saw your website—hope all goes well with your life. Man I hear you have a wife and kids too, that is big inspiration to me, I hope I am that lucky some day. God Bless.

TONTO: Hi Derek, nice to get a chance to tell you how much the platoon and I are into your CD Goodnight Soldier. It's the one we play over here at least once a day. War Dawg told us you grew up in foster care like we all did, but that's not the reason we like your music so much, we like it cause its hella good music number one. I like the song Good Night Soldier; it reminds me of my Grandpops. Derek you ever seen or heard that Oliver Twist story dude? That was my orphanage all the way. All us Native American kids there would be shorn of our hair, our language, our culture, our families; the purpose was to integrate us into the dominant culture. Kids would get so depressed they would walk out into the below zero snow and just freeze to death trying to find their way home. Some of the abusive teachers would call these dead kids Injun Pops or Injunsicles. The government said we go, we went, did not matter if we had family or not. My Mom and Dad bit it when I was young, about two, in a rez wreck. I was in the back seat. Child Safety Seat!—hell no, I was just running around in the back of the truck bed, with about nine other drunken adults. A rez wreck is too many Indians going too fast while drinking too much. When the pickup hit a semi, the whole thing just exploded, and I was thrown like thirty feet away, and woke up and wandered over to the accident scene. The cops could not believe it, my Grandpops said. But Grandpops always told me, *Tonto, you are alive for a reason. The Creator has good things for you to do.* So I had to go to a special orphanage for Native Americans, and it sucked big time. It was like Oliver Twist for real—rez style. It was in there I watched my favorite old-school television show which was the Lone Ranger and Tonto. Me being Native American, the Marines called me Tonto like joking around, and it just stuck. I don't really mind being called Tonto, actually I kind of like it, because if it were not for Tonto, Lone Ranger would not have his Mask, his MO, or the name of his horse—plus we NA's sometimes get tossed around a bit by people that don't dig NA's—and that dude Tonto, he always kept his cool, he was a classy dude, never cussing or acting the fool or becoming angry—so for me, he was a cool dude. Also NA culture is about helping your brother, and to the Wasichu, or Anglo culture, a guy is lesser when being a sidekick, but see, in NA culture, the guy that is the sidekick is the real spiritual one, really the higher one, cause he sacrifices himself for the good of the tribe or the cause.

It is the same as Jesus, really…except NA's call God the Creator. So your song, Goodnight Soldier, Goodnight Friend, its really mellow and it reminds me of my Grandpops. He wanted to take care of me, but the system would not let him, they thought he was too old to take care of me. Well all these thoughts, is what your music makes me think of. Hope your book is read by everybody that needs to read it, and get help. It's awesome what you are doing Derek. As we Lakota Sioux say, Walk in Beauty Always My Brother.

STRYKER: Hi Derek, it's really great you want to hear what we think of your music, because the platoon thinks you are the best singer on the planet. War Dawg brought a copy of your CD here to the Sandbox and the first time I heard that song Goodnight Soldier, I just felt really proud to be an American. When we have open mike night, that song is always the number one request. It makes me really proud to be an American when I hear that song. Doc Eagle said we are not supposed to bore the shit out of you. But just tell you straight up what we think of your music. Well the day I had heard your song for the first time was the first day I got to Iraq. While your song was playing, Goodnight Soldier, I fell in love with an Army girl, Pam. I fell hard, she was going to be my future wife in my heart. But what I didn't know was that she was engaged to an Army guy in a Stryker Unit. This girl was loco, she had me meet her inside a Stryker vehicle—we didn't get past a couple of kisses and her Army guy shows up screaming her name in the bay—sticks his head in and catches her ready to plant the fourth lipstick kiss on my face. She had on this real pretty hot pink lipstick, it was Diabolique by Dior…and most of it was on my high and tight…Derek, after the Army guy and I had a rollover (fight) we went to have a beer together, sold from this guy that was selling illegal at a Sgt. Bilko base bar [Translation: Army Entrepreneur selling smuggled in beers]. I reached in my cammie pocket for some green and there was Pam's lipstick. The Army guy and I couldn't believe it, either, but lipsticks have names! So that is how I know the official name of Pam's Lipstick. We hawed like hyenas and both about laughed to death. Turned out Pam was a big flirt and liked to make this Army guy jealous on a daily basis with the local jar imports. That's the whole sordid tale. Stryker Boy was then plastered on me by my platoon when they heard the tale of this. Now y'all know the whole sordid story of how I got my heart broken. So if you ever decide you need a good story about your music to quiet your fans when the electricity suddenly cuts out and they are about to riot, you can keep em subdued with this story about the dumb jar that lost his heart while your song Goodnight Soldier played in the background. Semper Fi, for serious Derek, your music is awesome. (Stryker wrote this to me before he was Killed in Action in Iraq, 2007)

IN CLOSING...

I would like to begin this final chapter with one of my favorite little stories about touching the lives of people who are in despair. I don't know who wrote it, but it perfectly describes having love and compassion for another.

STAR FISH

"One day as I was walking along the beach, I saw someone in the distance throwing something into the sea. As I came closer I could see hundreds of starfish that had washed up on the beach, and an old man who was carefully throwing them, one by one, back into the sea.

I asked him why he was doing this, and he told me that soon the hot sun would destroy the starfish that were on the beach, and he was throwing back as many as he could before this would happen.

I asked, "Why should you do this? Does it really matter?"

He picked up another starfish, then looked at me and said, "To this one it does."

-Anonymous

It's my hope that my story has touched your life, and if it has, that you share it with others in an effort to give them hope. If you know anybody suffering emotionally, mentally, or physically, and believe they could relate to my story, please share it with them. I believe that if you give hope, you are given hope in return.

Everyone deserves a better life. Remember, the tiniest positive action you take is a step towards a better tomorrow. Action creates momentum, and with momentum your life will never be the same again. So if you think there is a problem in your life, you're right. Problems are self-made. Don't think of life as having problems, think of it as having "situations." The word "situation" doesn't have the same negative connotations. Problems can seem insoluble, and may lead to inaction. But a situation seems open to remedy. Twists and turns make life more adventurous. This book has been about having the courage to never give up, no matter what life throws at you. If I Can Fly, You Can Fly! That is no joke, I have gone through hell and if I can do it, you surely can. So fly into this great open sky and achieve your dreams. The genie in your bottle is your WILL.

I still have many dreams that I want to accomplish. I have a strong desire to be a motivational and inspirational speaker to the adults and youth of this world. I also would like to be professional songwriter who writes songs that touch the emotions and heart of the soul. Who knows, maybe I will have my own talk show some day. Oprah, hook me up! I know I will get there with my principles of taking action. I hope that people who are reading this book might be motivated to find a place in their heart to help me achieve my dreams; so that I may help others achieve their dreams. If anybody out there has ideas or knows how they might help me accomplish these goals, drop me a line! Pay it forward, as they say. It is a cycle of love. If you help another, then that help comes back bigger and better to you. I believe that! The human spirit is simply an amazing force. I have seen it and lived it. Having genuine love and helping another only breed's more love.

Live your life with passion. Be curious about what the world offers. Be creative in your solutions. Be honest with yourself. Live with excitement and a sense of adventure. Be determined to never let yourself down. Endure the hard times for they do end, and they are just a blip on the radar. Be happy with who you are and share your talents with others. Be giving to those who feel like they're losing the battle of life. Even if you are completely unaware of your influence, something as simple as your attention may help them find new sources of the energy that is necessary to prevail. Be patient, life will happen no matter what. Make choices that are true to you, for every action has a reaction. Guide yourself with vigor and valor to the beautiful destiny you've dreamed of. Life is the pathway to your heart, and your heart is the pathway to your life. Dream big for beyond your dreams are the realities of tomorrow. Live ethically so that generations to come will know of your noble name. Above all, love. Love life, love yourself and love others. Where there is love, you'll also find the person who is in happy spirits and carries the joy of the world. May you bear the promise of never giving up and always loving as if there will be no more tomorrows.

"When you come to the end of your rope, tie a knot and hang on."

-Franklin D. Roosevelt

I humbly thank you for reading my story and I hope to one day meet you at one of my seminars!

CONTACT ME

You can contact Derek Clark at:

Derek Clark
4600 S. Tracy Blvd. #104
Tracy, Ca 95377

1-800-980-0751

Derek@iwillnevergiveup.com

Visit Derek Clark's web site at
www.iwillnevergiveup.com
And
www.neverlimityourlife.com

Derek Clark is an electrifying speaker whose message conveys a "realistic" mix of hope, encouragement and determination by sharing his sad and triumphant experiences. On stage, his passion for life and music will touch and warm the audience's soul. He brings humor and the power of music to help others change their life. They will walk away with a new focus and the confidence to overcome any obstacles in their life.

To have Derek Clark be part of your next event,
email seminars@iwillnevergiveup.com

For more information on Derek's products and services, please visit the above web sites.

I would love to hear from you. Please send your comments about this book to me. Please tell a friend about this book. Thank you.

INSPIRING COMMENTS

"On Saturday March 11, of 2006, my wife and I had attended a 'Gold Star Parents Luncheon' at a fine Italian restaurant in San Francisco. There was a gentleman there who performed a song entitled "Good Night Soldier." This was a very Red Blooded patriotic song that brought tears to our eyes, in part due to our own personal sacrifice. That was my introduction to Derek Clark. After a week or so, I called and asked him to perform in Jamestown at the 2nd Annual Tribute Motorcycle Ride for my son, in May of that year. My son was Killed in Combat Action on a cold Winter day, December 14th of 2004, during house to house "Search and Clearing" operations in Fallujah, Iraq, "Operation Phantom Fury." The Late Corporal Michael D. Anderson Jr., was 21 years of age, and a brave Squad Leader in The United States Marine Corps. Mike Jr. courageously fought in the "The Battle for Fallujah," which was very successful, and already slated to go down in Marine Corps achievements as one of the great battles in our history.

That afternoon event of March 2006 in San Francisco started a bond and friendship that has brought Derek and I to the same stage many times. Derek called me one evening about a year ago, and asked me a few questions about a new song that he was penning. "American Marine" was a song about my late hero of a son, and I am in fact honored to have collaborated with Derek on this track. "Semper Fi"

I have witnessed his live performance of "Good Night Soldier" to our President, George W. Bush. We have shared the same spotlight at a 9/11 commemorative event on the steps of the California State Capital Building on the 5th anniversary of the tragic Twin Towers attack. We shared a common stage at a "Salute To God and Country"; a Memorial Day Event entitled "Not Forgotten", for two years in a row, '06 and '07. We again have had a mutual stage at "The Sierra Hope Ride" in Sonora, California, back to back in 2006 and 2007. Most recently (Nov 1st '07), my wife and I were invited guests at a Naval Commissioning Ceremony on Coronado Island, Naval Air Station, for a Navy Mustang.

We instantly recognized the songs playing softly in the background as Derek's songs! I digitally filmed part of the ceremony and couldn't wait to share what I had with Derek. They played the same audio at the reception immediately following at The Officer's Club, on Base. I had to call him and rub it in that he had hit the big time!

Derek is truly military-oriented, and a supporter of not only our troops in harm's way, but the grieving families left behind.

We gain inspiration and momentum from gentlemen like Derek. My personal message to him is, "Your patriotism, love, and encouragement for the true patriots does not go unnoticed. We have many dark days, and you sir, shine a light that offers us hope and something to believe in. For that alone, we thank you. May God continue to bless you my friend".

With Deep Respect and Admiration,

Michael D. Anderson Sr., Angela A. Anderson   Modesto, California
Proud Parents of The Late Corporal Michael D. Anderson Jr. USMC
Killed In Combat Action   14 December, 2004   Fallujah, Iraq
Operation Phantom Fury aka "Battle For Fallujah"
3rd Battalion / 5th Marine Regiment, Kilo Company, RCT-1
1st Platoon, 3rd Squad
1st Marine Division, Camp Pendleton
www.cplandersonjr.org
 Veterans Day, November 12, 2007 "

"I just had to leave you a comment about your CBS News 13 clip. I watched it tonight as my 7 year old daughter laid in my bed trying to go to sleep. From the bed she could see the computer screen and as I watched the clip, your little boy reciting the pledge of allegiance, your little one yelling " I love America," and listening to you sing, I heard a noise behind me. I turned to see my daughter laying in bed also watching the clip and she was crying. I got up and asked her why she was crying and she said because the nice man on the computer was singing a goodnight song to her Daddy. Man!! Talk about emotional overload. I asked her if she was ok and she said she was crying because it made her happy that someone was thinking of her Daddy too. So for this I want to thank you from the bottom of my heart!!! Your song has touched not only me but my daughter who misses her Daddy so very much.

It has been a long separation and very difficult in ways that words could never describe. I find that the greatest comfort I receive is not from family and friends, because even though they say they understand they don't. It is from strangers like you who put into song what we feel. Thank you and may God bless you, your family and all those you love." - Irma Chambers.

"Derek. I needed a box of tissue when I went to the web page earlier. Two years ago this week I saw my husband's face for the last time as he got on a plane and left for S. Korea for more training and then on to Iraq. Six months later he was killed by an IED. Two weeks ago he was honored by one of his soldiers who named his first born son after my husband. It is people like you that help me realize that my husband died for a reason. He died for his countrymen, his brothers, and total strangers. Keep up the good work. It means more than you could ever know." - Jennifer .

"Dear Derek, First Of All I Congratulate You On Your Gift To The World, Your Song, "GOODNIGHT SOLDIER." You Have Touched Many Hearts, Including Mine And My Family's And Friend's. I Thank God For You And For Juana For Sharing Her Story With Me About How She Went To You With A Broken Heart After Returning From A Funeral For A Soldier (Lance Cpl. Brandon Dewey, From Tracy, Calif.) Who Was Killed In Iraq In January 2006. Her Comfort Was You Derek, When You Grabbed Your Guitar And Played Your Song And Sang To Her "GOODNIGHT SOLDIER." Today Your Song Is

In Many Homes All Over The World. You Have Brought Tears To Many Eyes And have Comforted Many Families Throughout the U.S. Who Have Felt Alone. You Have Made Us A Family With Your Song. The Love And Support Has Bonded All Of Us Throughout Our Country. Many Hearts No Longer Feel Alone." - Lydia C.

"On March 11th 2006, I was invited to a Luncheon in San Francisco with Move America Forward. This was the first time I was introduced to Melanie Morgan, a radio talk show host. I met quite a few wonderful people that day, and among them was a tall, very polite and handsome young man. A little later I found out he was a singer, and wrote a very special song. The room was fairly small, yet in one corner was a guitar, and couple of mics. It was before we were seated at a table being specially prepared for a few Gold Star Parents (which means we lost our sons in Iraq during Operation Iraqi Freedom). Over in the corner, this tall, young man took up his guitar and the room went completely silent. As he began to sing, my heart couldn't believe what it was hearing. The tears started to flow, uncontrollably, the moving, and powerful words, just rang through my body. I could very much relate to the song, as my son, Lcpl Travis Layfield USMC, was Killed In Action, in Iraq on April 6th, 2004. He was in an ambush that killed 10 Marines and 1 Navy Corpsman. Unfortunately, every day it seems as if I just got the horrific, devastating news of my son being killed in a faraway place. The song Goodnight Soldier touched and moved me beyond words. Derek's voice carried like melancholically, and his back-up singers voice was truly that of an angel, and their voices filled the room with peace.

Derek felt it, and wrote it from his heart. Where else could something this beautiful come from? I have come to know Derek a little better in the past couple of years. I've been to a few events in which Derek has also participated. I feel as if I've known him all of my life. Derek projects much love and caring for our Military, and especially our Fallen. They will never, ever be forgotten. We will never, ever stop speaking their names. Derek has added Travis to his web page video. Now also to his book. I don't believe in coincidences. Everything happens for a reason. Derek has touched Travis' life and mine for a reason. For this we are Blessed, and so very Grateful. Travis and all Our Fallen are missed and Loved so much. Thank you Derek, for such a Beautiful song and writing your story to be shared. I'm very Proud and Honored to call you Friend."

Proud Mother of Lcpl Travis Layfield
KIA April 6th, 2004'
GSM Diane

"I just wanted you to know that I love the Goodnight Soldier song. But I have a question. Recently a soldier passed away, and her family would like the song played at her funeral. They would really appreciate it. Thank you!"-Heather

"Derek has charm, sincerity, politeness & unending strengths to accomplish his goals. He is a successful composer & singer. We are so very proud of how he sets goals & achieves them. An example is when he wrote "Goodnight Soldier" and

222

then set a goal to sing this song to the President of the U.S.A., which he did do about eight months later. This album is so moving and inspiring that it impacts all those who hear it. We are truly amazed at his ability to overcome all of the physical & mental abuse he went through before the young age of six, to become the great man, husband, father, brother and son that he is.   Love, Dad & Mom McElhannon

"Dear Derek, I was referred to listen to this song and to watch the video of Goodnight Soldier from my wife. I was very touched by this song on so many levels. I am currently over-seas fighting with the 4th Infantry Division, with a wife and three kids back home. I have passed this song on to several of my fellow brothers in arms for them to listen to. I want to say thank for laying your heart-felt feelings out there for the world to hear. It takes just as much courage to do that, as it does for any of us to do what we do. People like you are the reason we continue to do our job to the best of our ability. People who share the same love, loyalty, and respect for this country that we soldiers do. I am proud to serve and protect this country with every fiber in my body, and wanted to let you know that it is because of people like you that I continue to do so. Good luck with this CD, I hope you go platinum. :) Best regards, your soldier" - PFC. Michael Walker, U.S. Army

"Dear Mr. Clark, my mother forwarded this song to me and it immediately touched me. It is Americans such as yourself that give these Marines/Soldiers who are deployed throughout the world the courage to do what they are doing. You may not fully understand the impact songs like this have on them.

It gives them the courage and the strength to do what is right. This is the type of song that is in their CD players on repeat in the middle of the night when they are lonely or are having second thoughts about whether what they are doing is the right thing. I will email it to my old Commanding Officer and Sergeant Major of my Battalion and have them send out a mass email." - Steve Hamilton, U.S Marines

"Derek Clark is a huge-hearted, strong and passionate person who supports our troops AND their mission. It's been an honor to know him, and celebrate his story."

-Melanie Morgan,
Talk Show Host
KSFO Radio
Chairman, Move America Forward

I was MOVED the moment I saw your video and the song started playing. And tears were rolling down my cheeks as well. I am a mother of two small children and a loving, supportive Army wife. My husband is gone to Iraq right now for a year. We pray every night, and every breath we take is for him and our troops fighting and keeping us safe, so that we can go to sleep every night and wake up every morning. Deployment is difficult and when my husband is gone I feel weakened. It's hard to stay strong, tears of sadness and fear are continuous.
But it is extremely inspiring to have people like you in this world to give tears of joy and inspiration during hard times. I am grateful for you. It's amazing that just that song alone inspires me to be strong and drive on! My soldier has to do it and I know

I can too! You have touched my heart and I am grateful for you! THANK-YOU! - JENNIFER

"Derek, I really love your song and website. My husband is active duty Army and so is my brother, and then I have other family who are in different branches. You don't know how it feels to have someone like you do a song like that. Keep up the good work and keep my family in your prayers." – Angela.

"Thank you for such a beautiful song that pays respect and honor to our soldiers. My husband is active duty and soon to be stationed in Kuwait. This song is an inspiration to our soldiers and their families" - Ann

"THIS IS ONE OF THE MOST INSPIRING SONG AND SITES THAT I HAVE SEEN IN YEARS. SINCE WE ARE A RETIRED MILITARY FAMILY, AND MY HUSBAND IS A VIETNAM VET, THIS SITE MEANS A LOT TO ME. THANK YOU DEREK. YOU ARE A REAL TRIBUTE TO OUR MILI-TARY, MAY GOD BLESS AND KEEP YOU SAFE." – SHARON

"Derek is truly one of a kind! I am amazed when I think about his tough childhood and how this self-made man has become so successful. Some people go through life using hardships as a crutch for why they fall short, but not Derek! It's almost as if having to work harder has built his strong character and undying will to succeed. We are so blessed to have Derek in our family and so proud to call him our brother! Love, Tiffani & Jeff Kelly.

"Derek: I cannot tell you the tremendous amount of emotion that hit me as I listened to your song to our military members. I was on my way to work from Vacaville to Sacramento, and quite frankly thought I was going to have to pull off the road until I could maintain my composure. Probably not a normal reaction for many, but certainly for me. You see I am the daughter and stepdaughter of a Korean War and Vietnam War veteran. I was an Air Force brat growing up in a small town in Idaho. My first marriage was to a military member, I was an Air Force wife for 15 years, and supported many during Desert Shield/Desert Storm and Somalia. I remarried and my husband is a combat veterans, USMC of Vietnam. He was in the first major offensive in Vietnam, Operation Starlite. Over 1/2 of their unit was killed that day, he watched many good men die." - Kelli

"Hey man that song was AWESOME!!!! that shows your true patriotism. Thank you so much. All of the other service members and I really appreciate it. There are very few people that show how much they care for us and their country, and you are one of those few. Thank you so much. From me and everyone here at Ramstein Air Base in Germany, thanks and God bless!!!" - Kenneth, USAF

"Thanks very much. I was listening to the song on the computer and it brought tears to my eyes. My son is in the mountains of Afghanistan for the next 9 months. I forwarded your site to all my friends. Thank you for thinking about our loved ones." - Azadeh

"At 2 years old, Elanah knows your September song word for word – if that doesn't make you a rock star, I don't know what does. It's pretty cute hearing her sing it, too!"- Amy Brooks

"Derek, Once again you have blessed all of us with your words, lyrics and music.
Goodnight Soldier is incredible. Keep on rockin with what's in your heart." –Alan & Kelly

"Hello Derek, I logged onto your site yesterday for the first time and after seeing that video and then my sons picture came up I actually sat here with tears in my eyes as I am now and I said a prayer. Derek, as a parent of a soldier in active duty in Iraq I want to take some time out to really thank you for caring enough about other people's children to show so much love and gratitude towards them. This is the hardest time of my life right now with my son on the front lines in Iraq. Thank you again Derek, much respect." - Brenda

"What an amazing song! I listened to it for the first time two weeks ago and every night I play it to remind me that we still have heroes! GOD BLESS ALL OF YOU!" - Dennis

"I have just listened to your song Goodnight Soldier. I have finally composed myself enough to send you a message. You will never know the impact this song has on me!! I am a mother of two soldiers. They have both already been to Iraq and both made it back fine. My 19 year old just volunteered to go back. He feels this is just something that he should do. I'm hoping and praying that they won't have to send anymore over there so he can stay home.

But this song is such a special song and I wanted you to know how much it has touched me. Thank you so much for what you are doing for the troops and their families. God will truly Bless you for what you are doing!! Thanks again. This Military Mom thinks you are a very wonderful person!!!!" - Janette

"Dear Derek, thank you so much for your album Good Night Soldier. I wept when I heard the song and saw the tributes to my friends son and other fallen. As a Marine Mom of four Marine sons, one fallen, three presently deployed to Iraq and Afghanistan, I wept with the emotion of your music and website tributes. I also worked with vets on PTSD issues for ten years, now I am working on an anti terrorism project that will create a university to train policy makers and community leaders in preventing terrorism. So for me, I really "get it" that FREEDOM IS NOT FREE. And your music sums all these personal experiences up in that one song. I cannot listen to it with out emotion pouring out in tears, but I would not have it any other way. Derek, you are an angel come to earth. I think God directly sent your music to Earth through your talents to keep all us military families and parents going. You are one of my heroes, and thank you." – "Doc" Alexander

"Dear Derek, I am sitting here crying listening to your beautiful son and are so happy that I have my US Marine son home safe and sound – he has been twice in Afghanistan and now just home from Iraq. We are so lucky but there are so many

families that are not as lucky as we are. Thank you for what you are doing.
Semper Fi." - Ingrid

"Derek, I owe you the thanks!!!! You are so AWESOME for what you do!, and I love your music!!!! Thank you for supporting our troops!! My son is in Iraq now, and has been since October of last year. I haven't seen him in almost a year. He will be coming home for some much needed R & R in July. I've already started planning his "Welcome Home Party." There will be well over 100 people there, all wearing RED, WHITE, and BLUE, at my request!!! Wish you could be there to sing for us!!! Keep up the AWESOME work that you do!!!" - Cherie

"Derek,
The first time I heard Goodnight Soldier was in your studio with my wife Amy.
It was you strumming your acoustic guitar and singing. When you finished, you asked, "What do you think?" Several months later you included my email address in an email that you sent to your closest friends and family. This email included an attached file, Goodnight Soldier. I shared this attachment with my family and friends, as did other people who received the email with that attachment, Goodnight Soldier.
A couple of days later we talked on the phone and you told me about the incredible response you received from all of the people who heard the song, then you asked me, "What do you think?" Last night, I came over to your house after you had returned home from performing Goodnight Soldier.

You performed Goodnight Soldier for some of the families of our soldiers that are currently on foreign land fighting for the rights we Americans hold so dear to our hearts. You explained how fulfilling yet humbling the experience was. You told me that it was a moment full of emotions for the soldiers' families as well as for yourself. You were shocked that the families asked you to perform the song a second time. After we talked for a while we sat down and read some of the postings that were recently left on the Goodnight Soldier website. There were times, after reading the postings, that you and I would just sit and stare at the walls. The only response we could muster was, "Wow." We talked about how we thought the song was a "good song." Derek, you don't make the front of page of a neighboring city's newspaper with an average weekly circulation rate of 59,206 newspapers for writing a "good song." Goodnight Soldier is something special. You reached into your heart and found something. That something is what a lot of people needed to hear. It is that something that a lot of people feel. Each of us through our daily lives taking advantage of our freedoms, and that's what it is all about. Being Americans, we all know that there are times when we may have to send our soldiers to a foreign land. Nobody likes war. Nobody likes losing their son, daughter, brother, sister, husband, wife, their Daddy or Mommy, or their best friend. Our soldiers and their families know the risks of going to war. They knew the risks when they signed up to serve our great country through the various military branches. Yet, they still felt in their hearts what a lot of people no longer feel. That this great country is worth fighting for and keeping strong. These men and women, and their families are the true heroes of this nation. Each and every one of them. The Goodnight Soldier website has received several postings from our soldiers of past and present and their families. It is obvious from the postings that you wrote more than just a "good song." You have received emails from people all over the world. From soldiers, their parents, their wives, and their children. They all share with you a little personal piece of their life. They tell you how Goodnight Soldier is helping them get through this war. One woman shared with you how she plays Goodnight Soldier for her two children each night before they go to sleep. Their father is currently deployed. Another was from a father who told you how special Goodnight Soldier was to him. He told you that that just hours ago his son's base was under mortar and missile attack. Derek, you wrote a three and a half minute song from your heart. You called the song, "Goodnight Soldier." You have eased the pain, even if just for a moment, of thousands of Americans. " – Mike Brooks

"DEREK, I am a Vietnam Vet and your song brought tears to my eyes. Thank You So Very Much for Remembering and Honoring the Men and Women of Our Military." – Marty

"I just read the article in the paper this morning. It brought tears to my eyes. Just earlier this morning I was on the computer instant messaging my son who is in Iraq right now. He just informed me that his camp was hit by two mortar rounds and a rocket last night. I thank God that he was not injured nor anyone else." – Vickie

"Derek, as a parent of a US Marine, let me say thank you for saying so well what many of us can't put into words. My son, Chris, fought in Fallujah at the same time Brandon Dewey was there on his second tour, and was one of the Marines in his Honor Guard when Brandon made his final trip home. When they escorted Brandon from San Francisco, Chris was absolutely overwhelmed at the honor the City of Tracy paid to his best friend. He said there were fire trucks and police cars with their lights on, and the firemen and officers were at attention and saluting as the procession went by. He was also amazed that so many people were out so late at night holding candles and honoring his friend. Brandon, like my son, is one of my heroes, and I can't thank you enough for the honor you have paid to them and their fellow soldiers with your song. God Bless you." - Stan

www.GoodnightSoldier.com is an amazing outpouring of the mans heart and it touched me deeply that this man who had no real ties to the military could write something so deep and emotionally tied to the men and women he was singing about. I am honored to know Derek and be part of his web site. I wish you the best brother (A title I do not give out loosely). Joe Toledo
SGT USMC 1987 - 1993
SGT US ARMY 1993 -2000
Operation Desert Shield/Desert Storm Veteran

"I want to thank you for your music! My husband is in Iraq and our best friends had just died there about a month ago! And it is nice to know someone is thankful for what my husband and so many other husbands do! Thank you for your music!" - Heidi

"Derek, miraculous is your song and tribute. For something to come out so perfect, it must have God behind it shining through. The world would be a better place if there were more people like you. You have touched my heart and many others. I also have a grandfather that served in WWII and received a purple heart.

My uncle fought in Vietnam and retired from the Marines. These are in addition to my boyfriend, who is deployed at the moment to the desert. What you have done really matters a lot. God Bless You and Your Family." - Jodi

"Derek, First of all I have known you for over 16 years now and I am continually amazed with your genuineness and charitable character. You are a great man and friend and a "True North Brother." Derek, your song so eloquently describes the thoughts and prayers many of us have had for our soldiers that we have not vocalized. You truly have a tremendous musical gift. 'Goodnight Soldier' is a beautiful song and I hope many may hear it and be touched by it as I have." - Dave Wilder

"As you may have seen, many of my fellow Marines appreciate the time and effort that you took out of your busy schedule to write a song regarding all armed force members. It's people like you that make me want to serve this country and protect what we all live for. I just wanted to personally thank you for the honor of doing what you've done for us. It's hard being a former service member and have people look down on you, or have people protest what you do because they've never been in our shoes, but to really take the time and do this, well boss, I appreciate it. Thanks again and keep supporting our Great Nation. You help us help you." - Junior

"Derek, thank you for writing such a beautiful song. Our family is so grateful to you for putting your thoughts and feelings into a song. It's so nice to hear that other Americans recognize what the soldiers do & what we as a family sacrifice so that everyone can continue enjoying their personal freedoms. Our kids love the song. They listen to it over & over. I want to thank you from the bottom of my heart for your song and your kind words to my husband. He was so touched & so excited that he heard back from you. Knowing that more than just those in your family and in the military community care means so much to him and all the other soldiers. My friend's mom listened to it right after she got confirmation that he was in the air and on his way back to the US from Iraq. His one year tour just ended. She said your song was just what she needed. Please know that your song is helping so many of us, especially my children and has touched so many too. I can't say thank you enough. God Bless you and your family Derek. Thank you! Thank you! Thank you!" –Kristin Walker.

"Derek, We would like to thank you for remembering our sons who have been lost in the Iraq war. Our son was a proud soldier." – Sheldon and Loretta

"Dear Derek, I saw a news story and went to your website to

hear your song and view the video. I just wanted to say THANK YOU ! THANK YOU !! THANK YOU !!! You have given voice to my thoughts and feelings and those of so many more who understand how blessed we are to live in this great, free land and have so many willing to sacrifice even their lives if necessary. We can never thank them enough !" - Dee

"Hey Thank you for the outstanding song. It brings tears to my eyes and brings back old memories." – Doug (Veteran)

"Derek, thank you for your moving tribute to our soldiers. The song brought tears to my eyes and brought back many memories. After the media's harsh criticism of our work in Afghanistan and Iraq it is refreshing to know that there are so many out there that support us. Listening to Good Night Solider and reading the entire website could not have come at a better time. I cried many tears this morning listening and reading Derek's website. It comforts me to know that someone like Derek cares enough to express his gratitude to the many soldiers putting their lives on the line for our freedom." - Millie

"Derek, I am a soldier in the United States Army. I am currently on deployment in Iraq and I just wanted to tell you how much your site and song mean to me and so many others out here and our families back home. It was very heart-felt and you really couldn't have done a better job. Thank you. Even though it may not seem like a lot, it is the small things that the people back home and around the world like this that mean so much to us as soldiers. It is what makes it worth putting on the same old uniform and boots everyday and going out there and putting it all on the line. Once again, Thank You and everyone who does even the slightest thing to help soldiers and their families in even the smallest of ways."

"Derek, Thank you for your moving tribute to our soldiers. The song brought tears to my eyes and brought back many memories. After the media's harsh criticism of our work in Afghanistan and Iraq it is refreshing to know that there are so many out there that support us. I know I will be going back, but with the support of friends, family, and wonderful people like you, we can all endure. I am proud of what I do and would have it no other way. Thank you again, God bless you and your family."

"Derek, Thank you!! Your song could not have come at a better time to comfort my heart. I am a military Mom who's son is currently stationed in Italy. He has been to Afghanistan and Iraq. He called me yesterday to tell me he is being deployed next month to Kuwait. Thank you for supporting him and all the other soldiers who are putting their lives on the line. I forwarded your website to him. He will make sure your website gets forwarded all over the world to all his military friends." - UNITED STATES NAVY MOM

"Derek, love the song! As a sister to an infantry soldier in the US ARMY, it is nice to know that somebody would take the time to write a song in appreciation of our troops. My Mom told me about your site. She absolutely loves it. Every time I walk into her office she has your CD playing. God Bless you

and let's all pray for a safe return for our troops."
"I heard this song for the first time this morning on the radio.
I was so deeply touched my eyes began to fill up with tears.
The name of the song is Goodnight
Soldier." I really had to keep my composure. I really felt grateful all over again to have the blessing of the many men, women and their families who sacrifice to protect me, my husband, my children, my family and friends every night while we sleep. The song is very moving and it is really special. It is raw, not commercialized, and I think that gives it so much reality and so much more love." – Laurie

"I love the song. It put me in tears. My cousin passed away in 2005 from injuries received in Iraq. His tank hit a road side bomb. He controlled it, pulled the others to safety and received 30% burns. He made it back to the States and saw his wife before he finally passed on. He is a true hero and greatly missed." - Jamie

"I cried when I heard this song, made me remember when I was there. Still am some days, but hell at least I didn't die I guess. I was the one who NEVER cried, stayed quiet, and stayed in the tent when I didn't have to be out on patrol or convoy or mortars were coming in or doing my other duties.
Thank you for this song"
– Ash

APPENDIX

PSYCHOLOGICAL EVALUATION

Dates Examined: 11/08/1976,   11/26/1976,   12/09/1976,
1/26/1977
Tests Administered:
> Wechsler Intelligence Scale for Children (WISC)
> Draw A Person (DAP)
> Bender Gestalt
> Children's Apperception Test (CAT)
> Make A Picture Story Test (MAPS)
> Rorschach

Case History

—

"Derek was born sometime after his mother divorced her first husband. For about a year, Derek lived with his mother and biological father. It is reported that the biological father was abusive to Derek. In 1971, Derek and his mother separated from the biological father. Shortly thereafter, his mother met her present husband and remarried.

Derek's mother is the daughter of an abusive and alcoholic father. Her first husband, whom she married at age 18, was also an alcoholic and an abused child. During the marriage, a daughter was born. She is now 16 years old. Derek's father was also an alcoholic. Derek's mother's new husband is known to be very strict with children. It is not known whether or not his mother or stepfather have ever abused Derek. They have had one child together, a boy, who is three years old.

When Derek entered Kindergarten, he had a difficult time adjusting to school. His behavior was so poor that the school requested he be withdrawn from kindergarten. This past summer, his mother and stepfather took Derek to the county family services agency and requested foster home placements. The parents indicated that they had no control over Derek and could not cope with him. Derek was returned to his parents, pending a court hearing, but the parents brought him back eight days later, saying they could not control him. Since that time Derek has been in two foster homes.

In terms of his early life history, Derek was a forceps delivery and his mother had to have labor induced. There was also an Rh incompatibility. During his first year, Derek had a case of anemia. He was toilet trained at three years for urination and at four years for bowels. He has a history of temper tantrums, eneuresis and encopresis. Head banging was prevalent during his second and third years and bed wetting was frequent throughout his first five years.

Description of Behavior During Testing

Derek is a slender child of about average height and weight with brown hair and eyes. He was always neatly dressed and clean. In the waiting room, he was observed as being quiet, but once in the testing room, his behavior changed dramatically. At first, Derek was calm, but when the testing began, he became fidgety. Shortly after that, Derek became distracted and hyperactive. He did his best to avoid tasks and when he could not distract the Examiner, he climbed all over his chair and walked around the room.

Generally, Derek responded to the Examiner in a positive mode. However, this was only after the Examiner had set limits about staying in the room and working before doing anything else. It should be noted that Derek did not always relate to the Examiner as a person. He asked her to do things for him that he did not want to do. For instance, he asked her to tie his shoe. Once, he picked up her hand and then let it go.

Every change in task caused Derek fairly severe anxiety. He would fidget or ask what time it was or tell the Examiner about his bionic powers. This behavior also occurred when the various tasks were difficult or threatening for him. At one point, the Examiner asked if he was scared and after an affirmative reply, it was discovered that Derek thought he was seeing a doctor. An explanation of the evaluation process relieved some of the anxiety, but not too much. Derek's behavior during testing appears to be fairly close to some of the reported behaviors at home and in school. Derek needed much support and encouragement to attempt the various tasks during the tests.

Intra-Test Variations:

On the WISC, Derek has a significant discrepancy between his verbal and performance scales. Derek's verbal scale indicated below average general knowledge, logical thinking and language development

Perceptual-Motor Coordinations:

In general, Derek's perceptual motor coordinations seem to be fairly good. The Bender appears to be immature. This indicates a weak visual-motor coordination. However, on coding, Derek's pencil marks are fairly age appropriate. A more likely explanation is that Derek cannot control his fine motor muscles for any length of time.

Derek's physical movements were observed to be well-coordinated and no awkwardness of movement was reported by the foster homes.

Orientation to Reality:

Throughout the testing, Derek maintained a rather tenuous reality orientation.
Before the testing even began, Derek told the Examiner that he had "bionic powers," and that he wanted to be on T.V. with the "bionic man." At times, Derek seemed unable to distinguish between reality and fantasy. During the CAT Testing, he physi-

cally covered the lion on Card 3 so that the lion would not see the mouse. Derek's reality contact fluctuated among the tasks. His contact was best during the structured tasks such as PC, PA, PA, OA and the CAT. It was 1 ? times worse during the DAP and the Rorschach Test, which are unstructured tasks. However, Derek gave some bizarre responses during the vocabulary test which indicated that he was not staying with the situation. For instance, for "Spade," he said, "It's a spade that goes skateboarding." Most of the time, Derek's percepts were either global or fragmented. His Rorschach Test responses were global while his CAT and MAPS Tests were highly fragmented.

Qualities of Thought Processes:

Derek's thought processes have a number of characteristics. Generally, Derek appears to be somewhere between the sensory-motor and the concrete state of thinking, developmentally. Derek's average math ability would indicate concrete operations. However, the numerous incidents of bizarre and fragmented thoughts make it difficult to discern his developmental level. One interesting note is that Derek has no ability to reverse thinking processes. Though Derek's verbal concept formation is very weak, his discrimination ability is fairly good. He was very observant and was able to point out and distinguish differences quickly. During the test, Derek exhibited much fantasy and delusional behavior. He also made noises that were sometimes animals and at other times were unintelligible. He appears to use his imagination as both a defense against anxiety and as a method of wish fulfillment.

Learning Process and Problem-Solving Modes:

Derek's approach to learning is a global one. He does not pursue one aspect and then another in an analytical method. He makes use of both imitation and trial and error. Even OA, his method of attack was a kind of random trial and error. He uses imitation to the extent that he could draw things that the Examiner drew first. However on BD Testing, Derek could barely copy the Examiner's demonstrations. For a six year-old, most of Derek's approaches are inadequate and immature. This is more appropriate for children aged 2 ? to 4 years old. Derek's DAP Test also reflects this. By six, most children are drawing whole figures. Derek could only draw a face and a sparse one at that.

His major weaknesses lay in verbal concept formation and language development. However, all of Derek's learning processes are interfered with by personality factors. He is highly anxious and is hyperactive as a result. He loses contact with reality frequently and perseverates, fantasizes and makes bizarre comments. This can happen without warning and in the middle of a task. The anxiety also manifests itself in sudden poor visual perception and in poor visual-motor coordination.

PERSONALITY ASSESSMENT
Identification of Nuclear Conflicts:

The source of Derek's emotional disturbance lies within his first year of life. Even prenatally, Derek was in trouble because of the Rh factor. Then, labor had to be induced, and the baby was

244

a forceps delivery. Also, sometime that first year, Derek was anemic and was abused by one or both parents. Therefore, the nature of his conflicts is a failure to develop any positive relationship with his mother, father or with the world. As a side effect, Derek probably was never allowed to fulfill his oral needs; at least, never in a positive, gratifying manner.

The failure to allow Derek the chance of a positive relationship with reality resulted in two things. First, he started to view the world as hostile and dangerous. Second, his helplessness in the situation caused frustration and anxiety which probably led him to withdraw. However, Derek was dependent on the environment for survival and therefore had to maintain some reality contact. This would explain Derek's severe anxiety which permeates his behavior.

In order to deal with his anxiety and growing hostility to his parents, Derek developed several defense mechanisms. He retreated into fantasy. He developed some self-stimulating behavior, which he apparently gave up after a while. He became hyperactive, because the anxiety was so overwhelming. Derek's poor relationship with his mother and his poor reality contact make new situations, such as school, threatening and anxiety provoking.

Developmental Level of Personality Development and Functioning:

Derek sees himself as weak and helpless in relation to others. As a defense against this feeling, he identifies with strong, powerful authority figures that aren't real, like the "bionic man." In view of his past history, his feeling of helplessness is probably fairly accurate. However, Derek isn't totally powerless. His eneuresis is an example of how he proves to others that they can't control him. More important, Derek became so disturbed and unmanageable that his parents got rid of him.

It is little surprise that the foster parents report that they have little problem with his behavior and that the eneuresis and encopresis ceased shortly after Derek moved in with them. Since Derek has never had a positive modeling figure, this adds to his difficulties.

When Derek expresses his impulses, it is usually in terms of oral aggression, aggression in general, death or sex. All of these provoke anxiety, but the aggression provokes more anxiety than any other impulse. When he expresses an impulse fully, it is usually blunt, brief and uncensored.

For example, on Card 4 of the CAT Test, Derek plainly said that the child was going to run over his mother and kill her. This type of response triggered severe anxiety. This blunt type of response was infrequent, because Derek generally blocks his impulses and instead gives a confused and bizarre response. Derek's controls are weak and frequently give way to impulse expressions in mild or severe forms. In general, Derek's hostilities are directed toward adult authority figures and seem to be expressed more toward his mother than to his father. The impulses themselves stem from Derek's earliest phase of development.

Derek's Super-ego largely controls Derek's impulses. Because of the severe anxiety that Derek's highly punitive Super-ego metes out, Derek has a rather diffuse conscious sense of badness and worthlessness. He has internalized the idea that most of his behavior is bad and must be punished if expressed. This would be the result of early abuse and neglect. As a result, Derek developed a strict Super-ego that generally tries to prevent him from impulse expression. When Derek's impulses break through, he is punished and feels worthless. Derek's view of punishment is severe and physical, as indicated by his CAT and MAP tests. Derek's self-ideal is probably that of an omnipotent authority figure who can do anything he wants. This notion comes from Derek's fantasies of "bionic" power and his identification with superheroes.

Derek doesn't appear to be experiencing guilt for his actions. Guilt develops during the analytical phase when the child is made to feel bad, because he hasn't accomplished what his parents asked, and he wants to please them.

It is suspected that Derek never got that far in development. By the time he was a year old, Derek had probably pretty much withdrawn from reality. Then came toilet training, during which his mother forced him back into the world. She also forced him to give up a part of himself. This terrified Derek and he started having "temper tantrums" which were probably more panic reactions than actual temper tantrums.

Eventually, Derek was trained, but he continued to have bed wetting and soiling problems. Also, he didn't want to get rid of any part of himself, and as a result, he began to hold his bowel movements as long as he physically could. His foster parents discovered this behavior recently and have been able to encourage him to move his bowels regularly.

Derek's relationships with his mother and step-father are obviously poor. Derek views his parents as punitive authority figures and as devouring. The relationship was so poor that Derek ended up in a foster home. Derek likes to watch T.V. shows like "The Bionic Woman" and "The Six Million Dollar Man", and spends a good deal of his time in fantasy. No one mentioned that Derek has any interests or play activities, and this author did not observe any either, other than fantasy.

SUMMARY

Derek is a six year-old boy with "potentially" average cognitive abilities. However, his severe emotionally disturbed state of mind interferes with his overall functioning and prevents him from developing along a normal pattern. During his first year of life, Derek was the victim of child abuse. As a result of both abuse and the accompanying hostility, Derek was unable to experience a positive relationship with his mother, father or with the world. He was also unable to fulfill his oral needs in a gratifying, positive manner. Derek withdrew from reality, but maintained a tenuous relationship with it because of his dependency on it for survival. He started creating a fantasy world and developed some self-stimulating behavior.

Derek began to identify with superheroes, and currently talks of having super powers. At times, Derek seems unable to distinguish between reality and fantasy.

Derek's hostility towards his parents and especially towards his mother caused overwhelming anxiety, which Derek handled by hyperactive and regressive behavior. The strictness of Derek's parents became incorporated into his Super-ego. The Super-ego requires so much energy that Derek is virtually left without any energy for goal-directed behavior. Based on the above symptoms and facts, it is proposed that Derek has Aretic Psychosis. Immediate and prolonged play therapy is recommended. The fact that Derek still has some reality contact is a good prognostic sign if treatment is begun soon. The foster parents are willing to take Derek to therapy. It is further recommended that Derek be encouraged to identify with reality figures rather than with fantasy figures such as those on television."

SPEECH AND LANGUAGE EVALUATION
July 8, 1976

"Derek was seen on July 7, 1976 for a speech and language evaluation. Referral was made because of 'gross motor problems' and his tendency to give inappropriate responses. Little was available for this child. He is currently in an emergency foster home. The home situation is chaotic.

Behavior:

The child came alone for the evaluation. He frequently requested to go home. He became restless quickly and a frequent change of activities was required, especially on difficult tasks. Cooperation was variable. At times, Derek teased and gave deliberately incorrect responses; at other times, he stated he was tired and wanted to return to his foster home.

Derek had a tendency to make hasty and often incorrect responses, which he corrected spontaneously. Perseveration in type of responses was also noted.

Behavior was immature. Derek talked frequently about guns, knives and hurting others.

Speech and Language:

Derek's speech was intelligible. Errors on later-developing consonants were noted. The child frequently misnamed items or gave related responses before coming up with the correct words. Example: door was a window and an airport was an airplane.

When asking Derek what we cook on, he responded with bananas and food. Upon further questioning, Derek responded to the question "What do you do before crossing the street?" with "Get runned over by a car."

He initially responded to the incorrect gender (he-she) but corrected himself.

Derek has confusion of word tense and does not differentiate between today, yesterday, tomorrow.

Test Results:

Derek scored at 31 percentile for age level on the Carrow Screening Test for Auditory Comprehension of Languages. He failed concepts such as pair, coats, the girls is not swimming, the dog is in front of the car, she shows the girl the boy, the boy is chased by the dog, the man has been cutting trees, the lion has eaten, and neither the boy nor the girls is jumping.

Scores indicate that the child is "below average."

Derek cannot read, add, or identify some letters. Neurological grossly intact but IQ-performance testing is compatible with a 4 year-old. The uniformity of the delay suggests organic "**Mild Retardation**" rather than psychosocial problems, but time will tell.

The results of this evaluation indicate that Derek would not function satisfactorily in a first grade setting. The child needs a program that would be supportive and provide success.

Recommendations:

    1. Further evaluation and observation to determine the child's therapeutic and
      educational needs. Derek would benefit from a complete neurological and
       psychological assessment.

School placement should be carefully selected. The child needs a program
      where he would receive emotional support, individual help, gross and fine
      motor training and language therapy. This may be available through an
      "educationally handicapped program."

REPORT OF PSYCHODIAGNOSTIC EVALUATION
County Mental Health Services
8/04/1976

"At the request of the County Welfare Department, a psychiatric evaluation of Derek Clark was conducted at the Guidance Clinic. The following recommendations were discussed with Derek's parents and were based upon several interviews with Derek's parents, individual play diagnostic sessions with Derek, conversations with Derek's foster mother and a review of a speech and language evaluation. Approximately 18 hours were spent in interviews and in preparation of the report.

To summarize the pertinent data, Derek is a nearly six year-old child who has been having severe behavior problems at school and in his neighborhood, to the point that his family is no longer able to cope with the pressures of complaints from neighbors and school personnel. The parents are at a loss to know how to help the boy. Derek's background includes extreme physical and economic impoverishment during infancy, and a father who brutalized the child.

Derek's mother expressed concerns that Derek's behavior problems were a reflection of innate characteristics inherited from his natural father. The speech and language evaluation suggested the likelihood of specific learning and language problems."

WHAT DO WE DO WITH THIS KID?

What do we do with this kid? Where do we put him? These were the questions being asked in the case files. Fortunately, my social worker did a great job in placing me with the right long-term foster family.

This following reports are from the social workers involved in my case, and will give you some insight into the struggles involved with getting me placed, and the state I was in soon after my mother gave me up.

8/19/1976
New foster home licensed for five emergency beds. This is a good emergency home, and I would hate to lose a good short-term placement. There is an adequate long-term mother, stern and rigid, and a father who seems loving and warm. I want to consider long-term placement for Derek, the mother's choice. She hasn't mentioned to county that she wanted this before. Might be too much for her to handle this shaky kid. She may only be committed through the first day.

8/23/1976
Foster home says it won't give up any emergency beds, and it already has five. If they can get licensed for additional full-time beds they would keep Derek. Mother says would rather keep all the children, most of who have been to an institution. It is

difficult to determine her motivation. She feels Derek would do better with her than elsewhere. She and husband are 59 and 62 years old. Mother is more physically able than Father. She says Derek has been no problem. Gets along well with others, has no behavior problems. When he first came, he had a forty minute temper tantrum, but afterwards settled down. Derek minds well, isn't hard to get along with. He is aggressive with kids, but not abnormally so, and is not particularly hyper, and is in fact a little slow. Derek seems attached to the family. It bothers him to see kids leave, and he has discussed long-term plans for school. Previous school problems are part of the reason he was put out. Talked to Derek. He is easy-going, curious, slow, not hyperactive. He had a brain scan. I talked to doctor, who ordered neurological testing. Will wait for test result before deciding placement.

8/25/1976

Placed call to doctor, Derek has gotten an EEG. He thought it looked normal but it hasn't been read yet. Derek has neural appointment set. Need more background history. Will send form to parents. Placed call to pursue placement depending on test results. May consider specialized foster home. Mother mentioned relinquishment during investigation and had questions on permanent placement.

8/30/1976

Placed call to Derek's psychiatrist. He had problems the parents couldn't tolerate. Was expelled from kindergarten. I saw the whole family. The mother was upset, step-father closed off and hard-pressed economically. Mother and Derek were beaten in previous marriage. Because of this, mother won't let step-father get close to Derek or involved with discipline. The plan is treatment for all. Parents wanted the child to stay with Foster Home, but the judge sent him home, it soon fell apart. Mother has indicated wanting the child adopted twice. Derek has had some evaluations. Shows immature speech, and may have a learning disability. He needs full-scale learning disability testing. Psychiatrist feels the child should remain in Emergency Foster Home until permanent placement made.

8/31/1976
Derek not obeying his foster parents.

9/15/1976
Met with mother, and picked up some toys and clothes for Derek. Also got record of immunization and Birth Certificate. Found out Derek has had no childhood illnesses except colds, and was taken to the doctors six months ago, where he had TB test, blood test. All results ok. Good heart and lungs. Child fell when two or three years old, had 2 ? stitches on head. Derek used to bang his head on the floor when angry. Mother states Derek has been difficult since infancy. Temper tantrums, hyper, and wanted his way all the time. He wanted to lead and control other kids. If other kids wouldn't follow, he would fight them. If he didn't get his way at home he would retaliate, breaking things, etc.

Derek would usually fight neighbor kids twice a week. and was a continual problem at school, sometimes hurting other kids, although not parents. He would yell at parents, but appeared to have more respect for mother and stepfather. Mother states that Derek's father was mentally ill and a criminal. She kept saying Derek is like him. The father had two other kids, one mongoloid and the other with leukemia. Derek is the cause of many family fights. The mother has only an eighth grade education. She has little awareness, is vulnerable. She says this marriage is ok, but the husband threatened to leave rather than pay for Derek's problems. Mother feels trapped, as if she needs to choose between husband and Derek. She appears to have very little confidence and low self-esteem. She appears unable to deal with children. Planning for Derek was discussed. She has talked about an adoption with the family, and has decided against it. She eventually wants him back, maybe in eleven months. She appears willing to work towards this, and has discussed therapy. She says they can't afford it. She would be willing to do therapy if they could afford it, but doesn't know if husband will. She wants to visit with Derek, perhaps every other week for a couple of hours.

9/20/1976
Place call to Foster Home. Derek loves school, reports no problems. Derek is counting up to ten. No word from his mother yet.

10/01/1976
Neural Test results: Neural grossly intact, normal for a four year old with IQ compatible for a four year old. Doctor feels there is mild retardation rather than something psycho-serial. He could perform skills but not up to age level. Not hyper-active, EEG Normal.

10/05/1976

Spoke to foster home. All is going well. School is fine, Derek looks forward to going. No bad reports. He works well with numbers and names. Foster home wants to keep Derek on long-term basis, and is willing to drop an emergency bed to do that. Wants to wait until testing is done though. Home feels he should stay as he has adjusted well. He is stable, and feels his age is not a problem. Derek has had no contact from mother.

10/14/1976

Derek adjusting well to class, mostly acceptable behavior. Fairly typical with some resentments coming out. This morning pinched a friend hard. He has easier time in small groups. Larger groups are too much, and he has more problems controlling himself. Better with older kids. With younger kids, he gets too emotional.

10/20/1976

Foster parents talked to teacher about Derek being a little trouble. They discussed school and previous home. Derek still likes going to school. Still waiting for test results.

11/09/1976

Foster parents have decided against keeping Derek. They've found that kids coming and going does bother Derek. He gets nervous. There is some acting out. When upset he doesn't wipe bottom and wets bed. His upsets are affecting him at school. He stomped on the teacher's foot, and was rude to teachers assistant, who is younger. Foster parents feels they wouldn't have the proper time for Derek. He needs home with no other kids.

No contact from mother yet.

11/12/1976
Placed calls to eight different foster homes. None interested at this time.

11/14/1976
Spoke to Foster Parents. Derek wishes he could see his Mother.

11/23/1976
Test Results in. Doctor says at least average IQ. Not dumb. Shows severe emotional problems and is hyper-anxious. I discussed with foster parents that I am looking for another placement and advised them to start preparing Derek. He messed pants for ten days. Is fighting at school with younger kids. I placed call to new foster home. They would consider having Derek for a visit. Placed call to current foster mother to arrange visit. She says Derek wants to stay but accepts not being able to.

11/24/1976
Picked up Derek for a visit. We discussed family. Derek says he wants a bike, puzzles, a camera and toys. I will check with the mother.
Derek seemed a little apprehensive about visit, but was not visibly upset when he met with new foster family and the younger kids. New foster home visit went well. He was delighted and told foster mother that he wanted to stay forever. Played with a pony, and was told about goats. He had a problem getting off mini motorcycle, but foster mother was firm and warm. She explained there were rules. New possible foster family feels

Derek is a smart child, is aware of things around him. The placement has been okayed.

11/26/1976

Placed call to current foster home. They felt like Derek had a good visit. Derek is ready to go, and likes his future foster family. The family thinks Derek will be happy there. Derek isn't nervous. A Sunday placement has been okayed. Teacher is having a harder time with Derek.

11/29/1976

Placed call to new foster family. They picked up Derek. He is hyper-active, constantly in movement, even in sleep.

12/03/1976

Talked to Derek's mother. She says she wants to see him. Mother gets teary when thinking about the new placement. We discussed long term plans. She still wants him to return at some point, and isn't in favor of an adoption. Says she is willing to participate in therapy but husband won't. Husband says it is Derek's problem, not his. We discussed the need for changes before Derek should return home. She said she doesn't know if she wants to go through with them. Things are fine with Derek. He does have emotional problems and is sometimes anxious. Derek was fond of his last foster home but makes it known he is going to be with new foster parents forever. Derek asked about Mom.

12/20/1976

Derek is doing well. He wants his chalkboard and eraser.

Derek is not slow. Does have problem with large motor coordination. He is clumsy, but small motor coordination skill ok. Has bad toilet habits and defecates to get back at foster parents when he is mad. He admits it to be the case. He is a very controlling child, and needs to have control over what goes on around him. He can be a difficult child but the foster parents are enjoying him. They are able to deal with him and are interested in helping him with his problems. His Mother sent a Christmas card to the foster parents but not to Derek. Derek refers to his mother and stepfather by their first names now. He no longer calls them Mom or Dad.

1/04/1977
Parents brought many gifts to Derek for their visit. Stepfather is functioning well. He put toys together and showed Derek how to play with them. He dominated the visit. Mother had normal interaction, considering the situation. She appeared somewhat out of it, and didn't show much emotion. Derek seemed glad they came, but was guarded. He has no questions about the rest of the family.
1/07/1977

Mother, Stepfather, and brother visited and were happy to see Derek. Foster parents say Derek is having school problems. Sees the problem as not being able to cope with kids. He is not ready to be in school if he can't compete with kids. He uses his strength to bully kids and also teachers. He seems to be doing better with control, and has more problems with neighbor kids than home. The foster parents are concentrating more on his weak points. That should change. There reactions to small things were too strong as well. They need to ease up on that. They feel Derek is growing up and changing too. Foster father feels his role to Derek is as a father, and did some discipline. But the discipline is mainly responsibility of foster mother while he is working. Mother would like to take him home for a visit. We discussed therapy for biological mother and stepfather. He says he won't go, saying he doesn't need it and can work out the problems himself, although he is in favor of mother going. They feel that because Derek was placed at their request there is no need for an evaluation of them. They see the problems as belonging to Derek, and are not willing to acknowledge their role in them. I asked what they would do if Derek smashed someone's car again. They didn't know. They thought he wouldn't do again. They feel Derek is getting close to an age where he can reason, but that may not be true. Mother doesn't appear to have any confidence in parenting or her ability to cope with Derek.

1/21/1977

Derek saw CDE Tester. Reports that first three times he saw him, Derek was nervous and frightened. By his fourth visit he was much better. Tester recommends play therapy, as Derek is hyper, anxious, and frightened. Derek does a lot of fantasizing, and unhealthily identifies with strong people like the Six Million Dollar Man. He thinks he has a bionic arm, an there are indication of abuse in early life, from six months to three years of age. Gross motor problems possibly due to abuse or restriction. He has ability and potential. Has dull verbal abilities but normal physical abilities. A lot of emotional anger interferes with what he can do. Tester recommends a special class for severely emotionally disturbed children. He feels Derek's emotional problems are causing him not to learn. Derek would like to spend the night with his mother. I told him that he can, but after a while. Derek calls stepfather by his first name, no longer calling him Dad. The family has plans for Derek to have one overnight with mother on April 2nd, then possibly every weekend if it goes well.

1/31/1977
Foster parents said visit with Derek's mother okay, and seemed like an overall positive visit. Derek was eager for this visit. He wants to visit overnight. He was a little rebellious afterwards. He enjoys having someone come for him, and talks about his brother as his little baby. He still refers to his stepfather by his name.

2/08/1977
Doctor Recommends play therapy. Foster parents feel this is a good idea. Derek is sometimes like a time bomb.

2/23/1977
Talked to Foster Parents. Derek is no longer vomiting. He is presenting more of a discipline problem, and becoming more aggressive.

On 2/27/1977
Derek visited home of natural family. After visit he had two of weeks troubled behavior. He was throwing tantrums and messing his pants, seemingly in an effort to get people angry at him. Foster parents are afraid of becoming angry, and do not anger

easily.

3/31/1977

Contacted foster parents regarding recent behavior. Also the possibility that nine year-old son is influencing some of his other behavior, rather than school or his natural mother.

3/31/1977

Talked to Derek's natural mother. She states she and husband have decided to give Derek up for adoption. They have been considering this all along. The last visit they had with foster parents they discussed Derek's current adjustment problems. They learned he is still displaying difficult behavior. He is a problem to his foster parents. The mother feels that if he hasn't changed, they can't deal with him, and aren't willing to deal with problems when he returns. Stepfather feels that it would create too much tension, and indicates he would leave the mother. Mother states that she would have too many problems if her husband left, and would probably end up putting Derek back into a foster home. She was counseled on whether her feelings were based on the fear of losing her husband. She feels that adoption would be best for both Derek and herself. At visits, the stepfather states there is always tension. Derek wouldn't listen. Stepfather feels the visits are a chore, and wishes to discontinue them. Does not feel able to tell Derek about the impending separation. Before, stepfather couldn't get a babysitter who would stay with Derek because of his many problems. He had hoped for changes, but they have not occurred. Foster father states Derek is still mean, headstrong, and physically strong. I have the impression the foster parents are tapped out. I asked about what behavior his school was reporting. I discussed guardianship, but the foster parents would rather have an adoption. They need permission from natural Father, believed to be in a San Diego prison or institution for the criminally insane. Derek's mother is fearful of Derek's natural father. This man cannot be trusted, and is physically dangerous. I don't want him involved if possible.

4/08/1977

Referral for adoption was not accepted. There are no homes available for a six year-old with problems that require long-term treatment. If foster family wants to consider guardianship, it would be accepted, and we will follow through with mother's relinquishment and a search for the biological father.

4/11/1977

Placed call to Derek's kindergarten teacher. Derek is doing well academically. He does good work, writes well, and has no real problems in any areas. He has adjusted, and isn't exhibiting disruptive actions. Derek generally respects the teacher, but sometimes tests her. He relates okay to the other students. There is no overt aggression. The main problem is him not getting involved enough in his own work, and getting too involved in other's work. Derek is getting a lot of teasing form his nine year-old Foster Brother.

4/12/1977

Derek asked about his parents at Easter and is still concerned with getting his bike from natural parents' home.

4/13/1977

Spoke to mother, told her that adoption is not feasible at this time. We discussed plan for guardianship with foster parents. Mother agrees to guardianship. She likes Derek's foster family. She wants more time needed to assess the possibility. Guardianship papers were signed. Mother was advised that she and family could keep some contact with Derek. There is some advantage for some contact, so that Derek can understand the situation. There is some relief that a decision has finally been made.

5/23/1977

Placed call to Derek's psychiatrist. Psychological Test results show a disturbed little boy. He is seeing Derek on a weekly basis, and has requested twice a week. Therapy will be long term. He feels foster parents are solid, and are interested in working with Derek. He feels the guardianship is a good plan.

6/07/1977

Placed call to foster parents. Derek says he is old enough to have a bike. I will call mother regarding bike. There has been no word from the parents since the visits. Derek doesn't seem to think about going home. The foster parents have had family-circle talks, and the kids could accept Derek as part of the family. There are some problems with the nine year-old foster brother. Derek's psychiatrist feels committed to Derek, and doesn't understand how the parents could have given up.

6/14/1977

Placed call to Derek's psychiatrist. Derek wants to talk with his social worker to ask why Mom and Dad haven't been visiting him. Doctor suggests discussing it in a way that shows this is not Derek's problem, but due to the parents' problems and worries. That the parents have too many worries of their own to be able to help Derek with his own worries, and that his parents feel Derek would be best in a home with parents able to take care of him. That they have decided as grownups that Derek needs help they can't provide. They felt it was best not to visit Derek now. It's okay for Derek to be angry at this.

6/17/1977

Received call from stepfather. He and Derek's mother feel they want to keep the situation as it is. They do not want to set Derek off course with visits.

6/20/1977

Derek asked how come Mom doesn't visit. I stated they have their own problems and can't help him with his. His parents decided it would be better if Derek were with someone who could help him, and felt it was better to not visit him now. Derek said he liked Mom to visit (because they went fishing). He would still like to see her. I asked how he felt about his foster family and living with them. It was okay, but he didn't know what it would be like in the future. Derek seemed okay. There was some nervousness, and almost tears regarding no visits. Derek wants his bike and training wheels. He got new Hot Wheels. I discussed guardianship with foster parents. They are ready, and feel it is the best alternative to adoption. They hope the mother visits. Derek was behaving the worst in the month after his parents stopped visiting. Everything is okay now.

Derek is doing well, is relaxed, and seems comfortable. They feel there should be no problems, but are in favor of therapy. School is going okay. There is program for educationally handicapped children. They will check out. If they feel it would be good for Derek, they will request that he be enrolled.